WALKS IN PALESTINE
Including The Nativity Trail

Welcome to Palestine…
…a new opportunity to encounter the past.

From the Bethlehem 2000 Project

'For centuries, Bethlehem has embodied hope in the minds of humankind. Whether we have had the privilege of visiting the town or not, its historic and sacred meaning shines like a lodestar in our consciousness. It reminds us of the bonds created by belief, of faith's ability to heal humanity, of the power of prayer.'

Kofi Annan, Secretary General of the United Nations
for the Bethlehem 2000 Participants Conference, Brussels, 11–12 May 1998

Dedication

This book was conceived by the Bethlehem 2000 Project Authority to enhance the economic development of Palestine. It is dedicated to all those Palestinians who had the vision and faith to create and support the project through difficult times, and to those we met along the way in the hills, villages and towns who gave their help and wished us well. We trust that, in its own small way, it will indeed contribute to acquainting visitors to the Holy Land with Palestine and its people.

Bethlehem 2000 Project Authority
and Di Taylor & Tony Howard

n.o.m.a.d.s

New Opportunities for Mountaineering, Adventure and Desert Sports

Greenfield, Oldham, OL3 7HA, ENGLAND
E-mail: tony&di@n-o-m-a-d-s.demon.co.uk
Website: www.n-o-m-a-d-s.demon.co.uk

WALKS IN PALESTINE

Including The Nativity Trail

By Di Taylor and Tony Howard
n.o.m.a.d.s.

2 POLICE SQUARE, MILNTHORPE, CUMBRIA, LA7 7PY
www.cicerone.co.uk

Thanks to all concerned

Much of the background for the Nativity Trail was prepared by the Bethlehem 2000 Project and by the Birzeit University IT Unit web team. In particular, we thank Hind Khoury, Rana Ishaq and Dr Nabeel Kassis, Minister of the Bethlehem 2000 Project. Also, Ranya and Marwan Tarazi (Head of IT at Birzeit University) who coordinated the Project, provided warm hospitality and were great companions on the hills.

We are equally indebted to Mark Khano of Guiding Star who made the initial invitation to us to visit Palestine and walk the Nativity Trail. Though they hardly knew us, he and his wife, Julie, welcomed us to their home during both our visits to the Holy Land. Mark was also with us for most of the walks, giving his help voluntarily.

Together with staff of the Alternative Travel Group and Guiding Star, both Mark and Marwan did much of the fieldwork for the Nativity Trail. They, and the staff of Bethlehem 2000, also gave invaluable support whilst we were working on the manuscript, doing everything possible to bring it to fruition for the benefit of Palestine. Sue Rockwell, Sue Heher, Anne and Henry Carse and others who originally walked the trail also contributed information, whilst the Applied Research Institute of Jerusalem made an indispensable contribution with their maps, in particular, Manal Daoud and Nader Hrimat, Assistant Director.

Palestinian guide George Rishmawi ensured everything ran smoothly as well as providing information and making the arrangements for our walk along the trail in spring 2000. Also with us were Guides Eli Asmari, Ramsi Ghattas, Kifah Al Fanni and Sami Abu Ghazaleh who, like George, were not only good companions, but added greatly to our knowledge of the Holy Land past and present. Reverend Andrew Ashdown B.D. and Susan Sayers walked the trail with us, opening our eyes to the Christian heritage of the route. We are particularly grateful to Andrew, who has since made a major contribution to this book, with biblical references and notes on biblical history. We also wish to thank the Islamic Association for Palestine and the Islamic Cultural Centre, Park Road, London, for their approval of our selected Islamic quotes.

The Sabat family in Amman, Jordan, provided their usual hospitality, making us feel at home en route to their homeland of Palestine; similarly, Adnan Budieri and family (also originally from Palestine) gave us their usual friendly welcome. Adnan, who is Head of Birdlife Middle East, also helped with information on this project as did Khaled Irani, Director of Jordan's Royal Society for the Conservation of Nature. Imad Atrash, Executive Director of the Palestinian Wildlife Society, and Mousa Sanad of the Wadi Artas Folklore Centre also provided valuable information, as did the Cave Research Centre of the Hebrew University in Jerusalem.

Our thanks also go to Buffalo, The Brasher Boot Company, Bridgedale Outdoors, Eagle Creek, PHD, North Cape, Tengboche Agency and Troll Climbing Equipment for supplying clothing, footwear and equipment for this project and our other outdoor activities; also to Mary Hartley and Peter Hall of Sansome Hall Architects, Milton Keynes, for their excellent and invaluable drawings and F. N. Hepper of Kew Gardens and Mrs Joan Petford for confirming some of the less well-known flower names. As always, we thank Dave and Suzanne of the Dave Cummins Partnership for their patient assistance with our seemingly inevitable computer problems. Also Cicerone Press for their interest in and unfailing support of the whole project despite troubled times in the Middle East.

Finally, we thank all the people of Palestine for their kindness and hospitality during our time in their country. We trust this book will contribute in its own small way to their future peace and prosperity.

Permissions

We thank the following copyright holders for their permissions:

Arab and Jew. Wounded Spirits in a Promised Land, David K. Shipler. Times Books. Random House Inc. 1986

Before the Mountains Disappear, Ali H. Qleibo. Kloreus Books, 1992

Bethlehem 2000 Project website, Dr Nabeel Kassis, Minister

I am a Palestinian Christian, Mitri Raheb. Augsburg Fortress Press, 1995

In the Steps of The Master, H. V. Morton. Methuen, 1934

Jericho – Oasis Town, Delia Khano. Guiding Star, 1998

Palestine with Jerusalem, Henry Stedman. Bradt Travel Guides, 2000

St George – A Holy Land Saint, Delia Khano. Guiding Star, 1985

The Community Tourism Guide, Mark Mann. Tourism Concern, 2000

The Historical Geography of the Holy Land, George Adam Smith, 1894, 30th edition, 4th impression. HarperCollins Publishers Ltd, 1974

The Nativity Trail. Birzeit University website. Marwan Tarazi, Head of IT

Scripture quotations were taken from the Holy Bible, New International Version, copyright 1973, 1978, 1984 by International Bible Society. Used by permission of Hodder & Stoughton Limited. Permission for use in USA and Canada kindly given by Zondervan. All rights reserved. 'NIV' is a registered trademark of International Bible Society. UK trademark number 1448790.

Other authors, publishers or copyright holders proved impossible to trace or to get replies from, despite our very best efforts. We thank them here for their works, the extracts from which give an added interest to a land already rich in history. If, unwittingly, there has been an infringement of copyright, we offer our sincere apologies.

Di Taylor and Tony Howard, May 2001

Text and photographs © Di Taylor & Tony Howard 2001
Artwork © Mary Hartley and Peter Hall
ISBN 1 85284 337 3

Other Cicerone Guides by the authors:

Walks and Climbs in Romsdal, Norway (out of print)
Treks and Climbs in Wadi Rum, Jordan
Jordan – Walks, Treks, Caves, Climbs and Canyons

Advice to readers

The authors and publisher cannot accept any responsibility for loss, injury or inconvenience arising from the use of information contained in this guide.

Readers are advised that whilst every effort is taken by the authors to ensure the accuracy of this guidebook, changes can occur which may affect the contents. It is advisable to check locally on transport, accommodation, shops etc. Also please be aware that paths may alter or be eradicated by road building, landslip, flash floods or change of ownership. The publisher and authors would welcome notes of any changes.

Cover photos
Top: *Looking Towards Jericho from the Mount of Temptation*
Bottom left: *Bethlehem Market*
Bottom right: *Monastery of Mar Saba, Bethlehem Wilderness*

CONTENTS

Old grindstone

Peter Hall

THE BETHLEHEM 2000 PROJECT
AND THIS GUIDE BOOK

Work on this book commenced in 1998 when it was conceived by the Bethlehem 2000 Project, which welcomes pilgrims and tourists visiting the Holy Land on behalf of the Palestinian National Authority. Under their auspices, the Palestinians recently celebrated the 2000th anniversary of the birth of Jesus Christ in Bethlehem.

The inaugural walk of the Nativity Trail, also a Bethlehem 2000 Project, was part of these celebrations, arriving at the Nativity Church in Bethlehem on December 4th 1999.

This resultant book is of dual purpose. In addition to the usual reason for a guidebook, which is to benefit the reader, the management of the Bethlehem 2000 Project felt there was a pressing need to introduce the outside world to those parts of Palestine rarely visited by tourists, pilgrims and travellers, to 'enhance the economical development of Palestine as a crucial part of building peace'.

This book is a project of:

Bethlehem
2000

Bethlehem 2000 PA
PO Box 2000
Bethlehem
Palestine
Tel: (9722) 2766244
Fax: (9722) 2766241
E-mail:
info@bethlehem2000.org
Website:
bethlehem2000.org

United Nations Resolution 53/27 on Bethlehem 2000, 18th November 1998

The UN recognised that Bethlehem, in the Palestinian land, is the birthplace of Jesus Christ and one of the most historic and significant sites on earth. It stressed the monumental importance of the event for the Palestinian people, for the peoples of the region and for the international community as a whole, as it comprises significant religious, historical and cultural dimensions. It further expressed support for the Bethlehem 2000 Project, commending the efforts undertaken by the Palestinian Authority in this regard.

FOREWORD

To celebrate the beginning of the new millennium and mark the anniversary of the birth of Jesus Christ in Palestine, the Palestinian National Authority launched the Bethlehem 2000 Project in 1996 to promote sustainable tourism. The project oversees the development of the Bethlehem District through infrastructure and urban renewal, cultural heritage restoration, tourism development and the creation of quality annual events celebrating Christmas. A programme of cultural, religious and artistic events was launched to revive and promote Bethlehem. Walking circuits were identified and promoted inside the newly renovated old city cores of Bethlehem, Beit Jala and Beit Sahour to show our rich cultural heritage. Some are described in this book.

For twenty centuries, people have been telling the Christmas story about the birth of Jesus Christ in Bethlehem and the journey of Joseph and Mary from Nazareth to Bethlehem. With this in mind, the Bethlehem 2000 Project developed a new Nativity Trail that links Nazareth with Bethlehem. Just like travellers in biblical times, hikers and pilgrims will be traversing beautiful but sometimes rough terrain, climbing hills, crossing deserts, pausing to rest in olive groves and sleeping in villages.

Di Taylor and Tony Howard have been walking and climbing in the mountains of North Africa and the Middle East for forty years. Their exploratory work in Jordan and concern for the environment and indigenous people is particularly well known. They were therefore a natural choice to write this guide. The Nativity Trail is more then just a trek, it is also designed to introduce visitors to more remote and beautiful parts of Palestine, and to the people in the villages along the way. It is hoped that in so doing it will contribute to all levels of the economy.

You will find walks in this book to suit everyone: strolls through Palestine's ancient casbahs and along the City walls of Old Jerusalem; pilgrim trails such as the Palm Sunday walk; trails to remote Greek Orthodox desert monasteries; rambles through valleys with ancient terracing for olives and vines; treks over high hills, and scrambles through savage gorges, even some opportunities for cave exploration. Whether you are seeking something different in old Nablus, a walk in the wilderness or a wild mountain day, you will find it in this book. There is information on the flora and fauna of Palestine, advice on environmental and cultural awareness and also biblical references and quotes. Indeed, if there is anything you need to know of relevance to walking in Palestine, you will find it in the pages of this book.

I would like to add my welcome to Palestine.

Dr Nabeel Kassis, Minister, *Bethlehem 2000 Project Authority*

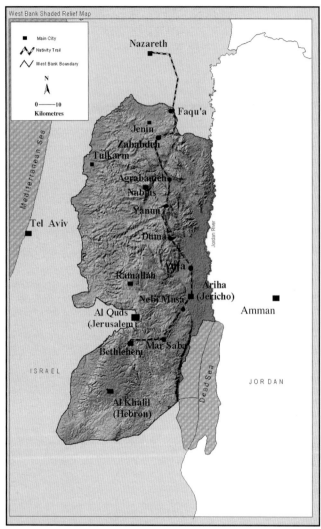

Israel / Eastern Palestine and the Nativity Trail

INTRODUCTION

ABOUT THIS BOOK

'Palestine is before you... Even in the barest provinces you get many a little picture that lives with you for life – a chocolate-coloured bank with red poppies against the green of the prickly pear hedge above it, and a yellow lizard darting across; a river-bed of pink oleanders flush with the plain;... limestone walls picked out with tufts of grass and black-and-tan goats cropping at them, the deep blue sky over all, and, on the edge of the only shadow, a well, a trough, and a solitary herdsman... But, whether there be beauty or not, there is always on all the heights that sense of space and distance which comes from Palestine's high position between the great desert and the great sea...'

The Historical Geography of the Holy Land, George Adam Smith, 1894

The walks in this book will take you through the rolling hills of the north, with their farmlands and olive groves nestled in green valleys; the wild, windy hills above the Jordan Valley with their panoramic views; the rocky ravines which lead from these hills to the salt-crusted shores of the Dead Sea, the lowest point on earth; and the bare emptiness of the Jerusalem and Bethlehem Hills. On these walks you will also see something of the wildlife of Palestine – the thousands of birds, visiting, resident and migrating, fleet-footed gazelles, perhaps even the shy ibex and fox, probably tortoises and hyrax and other small mammals, and possibly also snakes and scorpions.

We need hardly say that archaeological, religious and historic sites are everywhere, even in the smallest villages, from ancient wells and wine presses through to biblical battle sites, monasteries and Crusader relics. Even the architecture of the old Palestinian houses has obviously identifiable links with its biblical past. In these quiet villages you will also find something else to treasure – a warm traditional Palestinian welcome! In return, your presence will bring not just economic benefit to the people but, perhaps more importantly, opportunities for valuable cultural exchange – you will learn something of the problems faced by the people of this land, whilst they will benefit simply by your presence and interest in their lives. If this book persuades you to go, and helps you along the way, it will have served its purpose!

To this end, we have endeavoured not just to give the basic directions necessary to follow the routes but also to portray something of the

Peter Hall

The monastery of Mar Saba, Wadi Qidron

history and unexpected variety and beauty of the land they pass through. We have included numerous biblical references kindly selected for us by the Reverend Andrew Ashdown of Denmead, and also quoted liberally from the writings of nineteenth and early twentieth-century travellers, all of which we hope will add to the interest and 'flavour' of the book.

The concept originated with the Bethlehem 2000 Project, which created the Nativity Trail as part of Palestine's millennium celebrations, linking the historic Palestinian towns of Nazareth where, 2000 years ago, Mary learnt that she was to become the mother of Christ, and Bethlehem, where He was born. The Nativity Trail described in this book does not follow the actual route taken by Mary and Joseph 2000 years ago, as that is now lost beneath modern developments, but it has been carefully chosen to take you through a land that would have been very familiar to them on their journey. It passes by farmlands with workers bent at their tasks and ascends to breezy uplands where shepherds guard their flocks, black nomadic tents in the distance. It takes you over dry hills where ancient wells are the only source of water, with migrating birds overhead and gazelles running for cover at the sight of human intrusion. It stops in small villages, where the walker can enjoy the Palestinian hospitality – just as Mary and Joseph did. What more could you want!

Other walks in this guide explore Jerusalem, Bethlehem and Nablus. They wander through quiet valleys or visit caves. They follow canyon trails from Jerusalem to Jericho, and cross the hills of the Bethlehem Wilderness. They take biblical trails or pass by monasteries or places inhabited in prehistoric times. Like the Nativity Trail, they are as much a journey of spirit and mind as they are of body. You will find them challenging and fascinating and will leave feeling fitter and wiser! You need not be 'religious' to enjoy them – though you may learn much about the life and teachings of Christ – and indeed of the Prophets Moses and Mohammed and other great religious figures. However, although there is an undoubted spiritual aspect to trekking in Palestine, there are many other equally valid reasons for walking in this scenically varied, historic and interesting land. In fact, the rewards of being out on the hills, in clean air away from modern urban life, and amongst people who still value old traditions of hospitality are sufficient in themselves.

In addition to a rich biblical history, Palestine also gives tourists the opportunity to visit archaeological, historical and cultural sites that date to and beyond the times of the Canaanites (7000BC), and include the extensive Arab and Islamic period, as well as the colonial age. It offers walks and hikes in its extensive valleys and picturesque villages, as well as its deserts, hills and towns.

It has been an honour and a pleasure for us to work with the Bethlehem 2000 Project and the people of Palestine to help bring this guidebook to completion. We would like to conclude by extending the invitation that was originally made to us, 'Come and see for yourselves'. In so doing, we sincerely believe that you too will gain as much by walking these trails and meeting the people of Palestine as we have. As we said in our recent trekking guide to Jordan (and it's even more applicable here) 'Be as good to this land and its people as they will be to you and perhaps it is not too altruistic to hope that both you and they, and thereby the world, will be a little better for your journey.'

ENVIRONMENTAL AND CULTURAL AWARENESS

'Do no mischief on the Earth after it has been set in order ...'

The Holy Qur'an, sura 7, verse 85

Peter Hall

Islamic and Christian heritage, Old Jersalem – a view from the Ramparts Walk, R20

We are all too frequently astonished at the lack of awareness of many tourists concerning the impact of their actions on the cultures and environment of the places they visit: people entering holy places or sitting in Bedouin tents dressed in beach wear; picnic boxes and drink cans discarded from vehicles or left at campsites; toilet paper left protruding from beneath stones, names carved on the rocks. The list is a long one and gives our hosts a very poor impression of our society. For half of the world, Palestine is THE Holy Land, home to three of the world's greatest religions. Treat it and its people with respect.

You may choose to hike in Palestine for any number of reasons. You may be a nature lover, or interested in different cultures, or seeking a devotional journey – or perhaps you'll just enjoy the exercise. Whatever your motivation, this will be an enriching experience. You will meet the people of these biblical lands in the context of their daily lives, and gain a deeper understanding of the intertwined roots of the Christian, Muslim and Jewish faiths. You will be walking through the land of Genesis so familiar to Abraham.

Palestinian Christians will introduce you to their traditions about Jesus and his disciples. As you walk through the countryside you will hear the Muslim call to prayer from the minarets. Every day you will absorb knowledge of history along with first-hand impressions of current social, cultural and religious realities. Most probably you will come away with your stereotypes challenged and your perspectives changed, and with new insights into issues of justice and peace in this ancient and modern land.

One of the great joys of travel is meeting people from different countries – if we want to be accepted by them it is up to us to behave in a way that is acceptable to them. Make yourself aware of other people's customs and traditions, and act accordingly. Keep the good reputation of trekkers and pilgrims.

Cultural heritage

As guardians of the birthplace of Jesus Christ, Palestinians seek to protect, upgrade and share the treasures with which they are entrusted. The preservation of historic streets and buildings and the rejuvenation of cultural and commercial life in the old city cores of Bethlehem, Beit Jala and Beit Sahour have been central to the Bethlehem 2000 Project plans for maintaining and protecting the cultural heritage of the Bethlehem District. The most famous of Bethlehem's historic and religious treasures is of course the Grotto of the Nativity, in the Church of the Nativity. Throughout the centuries, many other religious and historic sites were built in and around Bethlehem, adding to its character. These sites remain a testimony to the living faith, which continues to exert its influence over Bethlehem and the world.

Cultural centres in Bethlehem

- Music and art workshops, concerts, and choral performances, weekly lectures, folklore shows and art exhibitions at the International Centre. Tel: 02 277 0047. Fax: 02 277 0048

- The Folklore Museum: sales of Palestinian hand-made embroidery and a traditional Palestinian lunch offered by the Arab Women's Union Club in Bethlehem (lunches upon request). Tel: 02 274 2589

- Traditional dinner with live music most Saturdays at 19.00 at the Arab Women's Union Club. Tel: 02 274 2589

- Folklore shows with a light traditional lunch every Thursday at the Good Shepherd Swedish School. Tel: 02 276 5898

- Traditional embroidery, shows of folk dresses and lectures presented daily to visitors at the Women & Child Care Society, Mar Nequla Church St., PO Box 313, Beit Jala. Tel/fax: 02 274 2507

- The Land Lovers dance show every first Thursday of the month at the Children's Cultural Centre. Tel: 02 274 2617

- Regular folklore shows with traditional dinner at the Artas Folklore Centre. Tel: 02 274 4046

Peter Hall

Traditional Palestinian home, Artas

Permanent exhibitions in Palestine

- Palestinian Heritage Centre Bethlehem. 8.00–19.00 except Sundays. Tel: 02 274 2381

- Artas Folklore Centre, Bethlehem. 9.00–17.00. Tel: 02 277 4066

- Museum of Palestinian Popular Heritage, In'ash el Usra Society, El Bireh. 9.00–14.30 except Fridays. Tel: 02 240 6876. Fax: 02 240 6544

- Archaeological Museum, Birzeit University. 9.00–14.30 except Fridays and Sundays. Tel: 02 298 2000

- Children's Cultural Centre, Bethlehem. Tel: 02 274 2617

- Crib of Nativity Museum, Manger Sq, Bethlehem. Tel: 02 276 0876

Cultural tips for the traveller

'We see people as we are, not as they are.'   The Talmud

The notes below are a modified version of a checklist from the Ecological Centre, Leh, Ladakh, India, another land of great religious cultures and traditions. The original source of these notes was confirmed by Tourism Concern as *A Third World Stopover – The Tourism Debate* by Ron O'Grady.

- Travel in a spirit of humility and with a genuine desire to learn more about the people of your host country. Be sensitively aware of the feelings of other people, thus preventing what might be offensive behaviour on your part. This applies very much to photography – do not take photographs of people without first asking for their permission.

- Instead of the western practice of 'knowing all the answers', cultivate the habit of asking questions, listening, observing and learning, rather than merely hearing and seeing.

- Realise that often the people in the country you visit have time concepts and thought patterns different from your own, but equally relevant.

- Instead of looking for that 'beach paradise', discover the enrichment of seeing a different way of life, through other eyes.

- Acquaint yourself with local customs. What is courteous in one country may be quite the reverse in another. People will be happy to help you.

- Remember that you are only one of thousands of tourists visiting this country and do not expect specific privileges.

- If you really want your experience to be a 'home away from home', it is foolish to waste money on travelling.

- When you are shopping remember that what is a 'bargain' to you may have been made possible only by the low wages paid to the maker or because the poorest merchant may sooner give up his profit than his dignity.

- Do not make promises to people in your host country such as sending photos when you get home unless you intend to carry them through.

- Spend time reflecting on your daily experience in an attempt to deepen your understanding. It has been said that 'what enriches you may rob and violate others'.

- Enjoy yourself, but remember that an extravagant display of wealth is insensitive to local people who may have to manage on much less money than you have. Nevertheless, respect and accept genuinely given hospitality – do not taint your hosts by offering money when none is required but discreetly establish first what is expected.

Community tourism

'The idea of community tourism is simple: you can help local people and still have a good holiday, simply by going on tours that involve local communities. In other words it is a mutually beneficial trade.'

The Community Tourism Guide, Mark Mann, Tourism Concern, 2000

For information on tourism and its effects on others, contact:

Tourism Concern, Stapleton House,
277–281 Holloway Rd, London N7 8HN, ENGLAND.
Tel: 0171 753 3330 Fax: 0171 753 3331
E-mail: info@tourismconcern.org.uk

For information on community and cultural tourism in Palestine, contact:

Alternative Tourism Group, PO Box 173, Beit Sahour, Palestine.
Tel: 02 277 2151. Fax: 02 277 2211
E-mail: atg@p-ol.com Website: www.patg.org

Guiding Star Ltd, Virgin Mary Street, Beit Jala, PO Box 1161, Bethlehem.
Tel: 02 276 5970. Fax: 02 276 5971
E-mail: info@guidingstar2.com Website: www.GuidingStarLtd.com

A Peek into Palestine. Tel: 052 685578
E-mail: neta_golan@hotmail.com

PACE (Palestinian Association for Cultural Exchange) promotes awareness of Palestinian cultural heritage and works (amongst other things) with cultural tourism towards lasting peace in the region and the world. Contact:

PACE, Samour Building, Nablus Road – near municipality,
Al Bireh, PO Box 841, Ramallah.
Tel: 02 240 7610. Fax: 02 240 7611
E-mail pace@planet.edu Website: www.planet.edu/~pace/

Sabeel (Arabic for 'the way' and also 'a channel' or 'spring' of life-giving water) is an ecumenical grassroots liberation theology movement among Palestinian Christians. Sabeel strives to promote a more accurate international awareness regarding the identity, presence and witness of Palestinian Christians as well as their contemporary concerns. It encourages individuals and groups from around the world to work for a just, comprehensive and enduring peace informed by truth and empowered by prayer and action. Contact:

Sabeel Ecumenical Liberation Theology Centre
PO Box 49084, Jerusalem 91492.
Tel: 02 5327136. Fax: 02 5327137. Website: www.sabeel.org

Sunbula, a non-profit organisation committed to social justice and economic self-sufficiency, provides a market outlet for village women, refugees and other groups in the Occupied Territories. You will find them in the grounds of St Andrew's Scots Memorial Church, SW of the Old City at the junctions of Hebron Road and King David Street. Contact:

Sunbula, 1 David Remez St, PO Box 8619 Jerusalem.
Tel/Fax: 02 6721707. E-mail: sunbula@palnet.com

The Lakiya Negev Bedouin Weaving Centre operates in the Negev Desert, a semi-arid region where Bedouins lived as exclusive residents until 1948, when the state of Israel was established and their lives changed drastically. The majority were forced to move from their lands and were no longer able to keep their flocks. To earn a living men sought employment away from home, thus women had to take on a more passive role. Life has been difficult, but the Bedouins of the Negev have never lost their dignity. They are proud of their heritage, and are well known for their hospitality.

Initiated by its community in 1991, the Lakiya Negev Bedouin Weaving Centre in Lakiya aims to revive and preserve crafts central to Palestinian Bedouin social and cultural heritage. Lakiya's contemporary ethnic rugs are handwoven from pure handspun wool by Bedouin women living in villages in the Negev.

There is a tremendous amount to see, learn, explore and experience in the Negev, and what better way than to stay with a Bedouin family. To help you experience daily life in the area of Lakiya, north of Beer Sheva, and the hospitality of its local tribes, the centre offers a three-day programme. Sunday–Thursday, 8.00–13.00. Rugs, etc, can also be purchased. Contact:

Lakiya Negev Bedouin Weaving Centre, PO Box 1588,
Omer 84965, Israel. Tel/Fax: 050 210327. E-mail:
lakiya@netvision.net.il

The environment – a plea

'The true servants of the most gracious are those who tread gently on the earth.'

The Holy Qur'an, sura 25, verse 63

The idea of the Nativity Trail was to find a route that would not only have a strong connection to Christ's nativity, but would also take the visitor to the more remote and beautiful parts of Palestine and be symbolic of the original Nativity journey. The route created crosses various types of terrain from low-lying farmland and valleys filled with flowers in the spring through to high barren, windswept summits and hot, dry sub-sea-level desert. Some of the walks follow country lanes or existing trails. Others make their own way across the land. Few of these ways other than the tracks between villages are frequently walked.

In the introduction to our recent guide to Jordan – Walks, Treks, Caves, and Canyons (Cicerone Press) – we debated the dilemma usually faced by guidebook writers: do we say nothing and hope these places remain 'undiscovered' and pristine, or do we tell all and risk the hidden jewels being destroyed so that others can share our discoveries and the local people can benefit from their visits? No such soul-searching was necessary for this guide! It was written as much for the people of Palestine as about the land of Palestine. It is our sincere hope that it will bring walkers to experience the warm good nature of the former, and the fascinating variety of the latter. Nevertheless, when we walk 'off the beaten track' we cannot be complacent about our

Mary Hartley

Star of Bethlehem

impact on the people and the land, both of which will inevitably be changed. It is up to us all to make our impact a positive one. We consequently hope that readers of this guide will act in a way that will be a credit to them. You should find little or no litter on the trails in this book. The people you will meet will inevitably be welcoming and friendly. Please do everything you can to keep it this way. Spend time with them, learn from them, enjoy their company, share your experiences, have fun, take care and tread gently!

Environmental tips for the traveller

'The world is green and beautiful and Allah has appointed you as his stewards over it. He sees how you acquit yourselves.'

Sayings of the Prophet Mohammed

Below is an amalgam of the International Union of Alpine Associations Mountain Code, the British Mountaineering Council's conservation booklet – Tread Lightly, and the Himalayan Tourist Code published by Tourism Concern, sponsored by The Independent and Rough Guides publications. By following these simple guidelines, you can help preserve the unique environment of Palestine.

- Observe any locally approved restrictions and access agreements and avoid any actions that might endanger access.

- Limit desertification – make no open fires and discourage others from doing so on your behalf.

- Remove litter, burn or bury paper and carry out all non-degradable litter. Keep campsites clean. Graffiti are permanent examples of environmental pollution.

- Keep local water clean and avoid using pollutants such as detergents in streams, wells or springs. If no toilet facilities are available, make sure you are far away from water sources, and bury waste. Burn toilet paper or use water instead.

- Do not disturb nesting birds or other wildlife and respect sites of historical, geological or other scientific interest. Plants should be left to flourish in their natural environment – do not take cuttings, seeds and roots. It is illegal in Nature Reserves and International Birdlife Areas and bad practice elsewhere.

- Do not disturb livestock or damage crops or vegetation.

- Avoid actions that cause unnecessary erosion (such as taking shortcuts on footpaths). Wear lightweight boots or trainers and tread carefully, especially in descent.

- Do not leave unnecessary waymarks.

- Help your guides and companions to follow conservation measures.

For information on mountain tourism and the ethics and responsibilities of trekkers and climbers, contact:

The British Mountaineering Council,
Burton Rd, Manchester M20 2BB, ENGLAND.
Tel: 0161 445 4747. Fax: 0161 445 4500. E-mail: info@thebmc.co.uk

or your national mountaineering or trekking organisation.

For information on environmental action in the Holy Land, contact:

The Palestinian Ministry of Environmental Affairs (MEnA), Hebron
E-mail: menah@palnet.com

Applied Research Institute – Jerusalem (ARIJ)
Caritas Street, PO Box 860, Bethlehem, Palestine
Tel: 02 2741889 Fax: 02 2776966
E-mail: postmaster@arij.org Website: www.arij.org

Friends of the Earth, Middle East (FOEME)
PO Box 9341, Amman 11191, Jordan
Tel: 009626 6 5866602 Fax: 00962 6 5866604
E-mail: foeme@go.com.jo Website: www.foeme.org

Ecopeace, a consortium of Egyptian , Israeli, Jordanian and Palestinian environmental non-governmental organisations working jointly to promote sustainable development in the Middle East:

2 El Akhtal St, PO Box 5532, East Jerusalem 97400
Tel: 02 626 0841. Fax: 02 626 0840. E-mail: ecopeace@netvision.net.il

Royal Society for the Conservation of Nature (RSCN)
PO Box 6354, Amman, Jordan
Tel: 00962 6 5337931. E-mail: rscn@nets.com.jo

Society for the Protection of Nature in Israel (SPNI)
13 Heleni Hamalka St, PO Box 930, Jerusalem 91008
Tel: 02 624 4605/625 2357

The Palestinian Wild Life Society (PWLS)
PO Box 89 Beit Sahour, Palestine
E-mail: wildlife@palnet.com Website: www.wildlife-pal.org

There are two types of Conservation Areas in the Occupied Territories – Nature Reserves declared by SPNI under Israeli settlements criteria, and International Birdlife Areas (IBAs) approved by PWLS in line with IUCN and UNESCO criteria. Some (for example Wadi Qelt) come under both categories. It is hoped that in the future all areas will be solely under PWLS jurisdiction.

The Palestinian Wildlife Society

The PWLS was founded in autumn 1998 and has clear and strategic objectives regarding environmental concepts, conservation of nature and biodiversity. It has already proven effective in raising environmental awareness throughout different sections in the Palestinian territories. Its mission is 'Conservation and enhancement of Palestinian Biodiversity and Wildlife' and its conservation philosophy is 'Think globally, act locally'.

PWLS believes that conservation education is the main pillar in the conservation movement of any country, therefore it has worked intensively in the field of awareness and education with different sections. One of its successes was the inclusion of environment in the national education curriculum of the Ministry of Education in Palestine. It was also part of the National Biodiversity Strategy and Action Plan for Palestine with the Palestinian Environmental Authority.

PWLS encourages the development of eco-tourism and is fully supportive of this guidebook project, which it hopes will introduce visitors to the bio-diversity of Palestine. It co-operates with three main organisations working in different districts and locations in Palestine:

- Palestinian Organisation for Protection of Environment (Jenin)
- Green Peace Association (Deir Al-Baleh, Gaza) and
- Palestinian Agriculture Relief Committee (PARC)

as well as various international organisations.

The land and wildlife of Palestine

The area covered by this guide includes four different eco-systems.

- The 'Mediterranean zone' of forests, maquis and scrub which extends across the north of the country, including much of the Nablus Hills and the hills of Jerusalem, Bethlehem and Hebron.

- The 'Irano-Turanian zone' or 'Oriental steppe' along the Jordan Valley and its fringing Bethlehem Wilderness.

- The hotter, drier 'Sahara-Arabian zone' further east and south near the Dead Sea.

- The 'Sudanian–Zambesian zone' found in oases and river beds.

These substantial local climatic variations are largely due to the extensive differential in heights from the lowest point at the Dead Sea, 400m below sea level, to the mountain tops at close to 1000m. Other contributory factors include the different soil types (rich agricultural soil to desert sand) and the varying rainfall levels – from a mean annual rainfall of 50mm in the Jordan Rift Valley to nearer 800mm in the north and west. Run-off from the mountains is high and much water soaks into the valley floors. Consequently, the vegetation there is much denser than would be expected from the low rainfall. All of this creates multiple wildlife habitats and complex ecology with many different species of flora and fauna in a surprisingly varied and beautiful country. It also creates an environment that needs to be carefully protected.

Palestine is a particular delight in spring when the fields and hills are dotted with flowering poppies, anemones, mustard, mountain tulips, chrysanthemum, daisies and other plants too numerous to mention. Here and there are delicately veined iris, or aloes and cactus. Carpets of scented herbs such as sage, thyme and camomile crush underfoot. Blackberry and other fruits cling to ancient walls. Oak, carob, willow and the ubiquitous olive trees cast their welcome shade. Even in autumn, when Palestine is a dry golden-brown, some plants are still flowering in readiness for winter rains.

Wildlife is equally varied, but perhaps less obvious. Insects, spiders and other small creatures such as lizards, gerbils and desert rodents are everywhere (but not too many nasties like mosquitoes and sand flies). Creatures that prey on them, such as scorpions and snakes, are fairly common but seldom seen (most notoriously the Palestinian Viper and Horned Viper). They will avoid man, but take care in thick vegetation or rocky terrain. Rabbits, porcupines, mongoose and the few scattered herds of ibex and gazelles are equally shy, though hedgehogs, tortoises and foxes are fairly common, and rock hyrax will be seen scurrying amongst canyon cliffs. Interestingly, crabs, frogs and fishes are found, even in the most remote desert streams and oases.

Perhaps most breathtaking of all are the millions of birds that pass over Palestine on their spring and autumn migrations. The rich variety of habitat, combined with a direct migration route between Africa, Europe, and Asia up the Jordan Valley, makes the area a key region for migrating, visiting and resident birds. Around 500

Mary Hartley

Palestinian Camomile

species have been recorded with about 500 million migrants passing annually. In the fertile Jezreel Valley south-east of Nazareth there are about 14 globally and regionally threatened bird species, either resident, visiting or passing through. There are approximately 400 species of bird in this small area, including thousands of breeding, wintering or migrating birds such as Ibis, Egrets, White Stork, Lesser Spotted Eagle and Levant Sparrow Hawk. You may also see the Black Francolin and rare Pygmy Cormorant nesting here.

Further south, in the hills above the Jordan Valley and around Jericho or in the hills west of the Dead Sea, raptors, cranes and storks may be seen in large numbers. There are also four globally and regionally threatened species around Jericho, whilst the nearby desert hills support a dozen globally or regionally threatened birds amongst their surprisingly large range of species. The Fan-Tailed Raven and Tristram's Grackle will be seen here, also finches, shrikes, desert partridges, warblers, falcons, eagles and many other species. For additional information, contact PWLS (see above) who are the Birdlife International representative in Palestine. Or, information may also be obtained directly from:

Bird Life International, P.O. Box 6354, Amman 11183, JORDAN
Tel: 009626 5337931/2 or 5347733. Fax: 009626 53347411
E-mail: birdlife@nol.com.jo

ABOUT PALESTINE

The Palestinians

'Until you've experienced it yourself, the Palestinian's extraordinary kindness and genuine concern for foreign visitors does indeed seem either miraculous or fantastical.'

Palestine with Jerusalem, Henry Stedman, Bradt Travel Guide, 2000

The human history of the land goes back over one million years – some of the routes in this book visit prehistoric sites of unique relevance to man's history. Archaeologists have traced Palestinian origins back over 5000 years to the time of the Canaanites from Eastern Arabia and the Philistines or 'sea-people' who arrived later from the Mediterranean in the third millennium BC. It was not until about 2000 years later that the Hebrews arrived on the scene, prior to 1000BC.

The image of the Philistines as uncultured (a dictionary definition) has its origins in the Bible, but since the Israelites were at war with them for two centuries it is hardly surprising that they wrote about them so disparagingly. Archaeology is now revealing a different story: it seems they were cosmopolitan craftsmen excelling in fine pottery. Since those Old Testament times, many other races and civilisations have passed through the land and contributed to its history, some intermingling peacefully with its original inhabitants, others belligerently.

The Palestinians of today are an Arabic people, though the Ancient Egyptians, Israelites, Assyrians, Persians, Greeks, Romans, European Crusaders and others inevitably left their mark both on the land and the people. There have been many rulers and empires here including pagan, Jewish, Roman, Christian Byzantine, Islamic Ommayads, Mamelukes, Ottomans and, in the first half of the last century, the British Mandate. All of which, of course, had its effect on the resident population:

'As each civilisation waned and lost its hold, its heritage was assimilated within the civilisation that followed. Modern Palestinian cultural identity has taken shape under the influence of the various civilisations that reigned over the land of Palestine. The various Semitic and non-Semitic inhabitants of Palestine were first unified ideologically through Christianity. Between the seventh and ninth centuries, when the majority of Palestinians converted to Islam and exchanged their various dialects for the Arabic language, the language of the Qur'an and that of the Moslem rulers, the seeds for a modern Palestinian cultural identity were sown.'

Before the Mountains Disappear, Ali H. Qleibo,1992

Despite these seemingly constant upheavals, evidence of the Palestinian peoples' continual occupation of the land can be seen everywhere. On many of the walks in this book you will see ancient terracing, which is still in use today and whose origins date back to Canaanite times (R17 is typical). Some of the gnarled olive trees so lovingly nurtured by the Palestinians are said date from the time of Christ. They are symbolic of the Palestinians – deep rooted in the soil, resilient in adverse conditions, and even when cut down, they grow again. The olive groves are almost sacred to Palestinians and are the hub of village life:

> 'It was an inexhaustible joy to all of them to behold the fruits of their own labor. The whole family would move out to the fields every day; father, mother, sons, and daughters all participated in the work as well as the harvest. During harvest time the family even spent their nights in a cave on their land. They would light a fire in the evening and sing songs, tell stories, and finish with a small devotional service. When the harvest was over, the family returned to Bethlehem, where they sold most of their crops, allowing them to live on their earnings from the sale.'

I am a Palestinian Christian, Mitri Raheb, 1995

Bedouin shepherdess on Palestine's Eastern Hills

Sadly, Israeli settlers and military have destroyed many of the ancient olive groves, physically uprooting about 100,000 trees, even taking the land itself without the permission of, or any compensation to, its rightful owners.

As evidence of their historic longevity, many of the old villages also have names that go back to Canaanite and biblical times. Ancient trails can still be found winding over the hills from village to village – some are part of the Nativity Trail and the other walks described in this book.

With the 'naqba' of 1948 and the war of 1967, many Palestinians fled or were evicted, becoming refugees or making new lives for themselves abroad. There are now twice as many Palestinians living outside the Occupied Territories as there are within, and many of them are refugees. At the time of writing, only about 10% of Gaza and the West Bank (which is only about 22% of historical Palestine) are under full Palestinian control. Of those still resident in the Occupied Territories, there are about two and half million Muslims and a diminishing population of about 50,000 Christians. Included in the Muslim population are about 20,000 Bedouin, who have a particularly hard time as their rights to the land as indigenous people are totally ignored by Israel.

Despite, or perhaps because of their problems, the Palestinians have proven themselves a warm-hearted people as ready to forget old differences as to struggle with current ones. We well recall someone saying to us, on discovering we were British, 'You gave away my country, but you are welcome. Come in and have some tea.' We can assure you that wherever you go in Palestine, you too will be received with a warm, time-honoured Palestinian welcome.

Recommended reading: William Dalrymple's *From the Holy Mountain* and the books quoted above by Ali H. Qleibo and Mitri Raheb.

Archaeological periods in Palestine

Palaeolithic	1,500,000 – 8300 BC
Neolithic (including Canaanites)	8300 – 3150 BC
Bronze Age (including Philistines)	3150 – 1250 BC
Iron Age (including Hebrews)	1250 – 587 BC
Babylonian and Persian	586 – 332 BC
Hellenistic	332 – 152 BC
Roman	37BC – 324 AD

For historical and archaeological info, contact:

Archaeological Museum at Birzeit University. Tel: 02 298 2000.
9.00 – 14.30 except for Fridays and Sundays

British School of Archaeology, Sheikh Jarrah, PO Box19283
Jerusalem. Tel: 02 582 8101. Fax: 02 532 3844
E-mail: bsaj@vms.huji.ac.il
Website: http:/britac3.britac.ac.uk/institutes/jerus/index.html

For up-to-date info on Palestine contact ARIJ. (See above,
'Environmental tips for the traveller'.)

Palestinian dress

Almost uniquely in the Near East, the Palestinians – especially the older
women – continue to wear their traditional dress for everyday life, at
home, in the streets and markets, or in the fields.

The distinctive full-length dress has multi-coloured embroidery on
the chest and is fastened at the waist by a belt; there are also
embroidered panels down the dress. Dependent on the season it may
be worn with a short over-jacket. The traditional head piece decorated
with coins and held in place with a decorative 'chin-chain' is still
occasionally seen. (When we were helping with the olive picking in
October 2000 it was a delight to see the 'grandmother' wearing the
full traditional costume.) Occasionally you may also see elderly women
with facial tattoos; perhaps more common amongst the Bedouin, but
this custom is all but gone.

The distinctive men's costume largely disappeared during the latter
half of the 20th century. The turban, *tarbush* ('Turkish' felt hat) and
striped coats are seldom seen. The *kaffiyeh* or headscarf of the Bedouin
is still very common; the black and white check popularised by Yasser
Arafat is a strong symbol of Palestinian nationality. The red and white
check, more often seen in Jordan, is also popular. Plain white tends to
be the prerogative of the older men.

Samples of traditional hand embroidery can be purchased in the
markets and craft shops (see R16, 20 and 31). Additionally, a good
place to shop for embroidery and crafts in Jerusalem is Sunbula, a non-
profit organisation committed to social justice and economic self-
sufficiency. (See the section 'Community tourism', above, for details.)

**Recommended reading: *Palestinian Costume*, Shelagh Weir,
British Museum Press, 1989. Also a booklet from Sunbula:
Embroidering a Life: Palestinian Women and Embroidery,
Elizabeth Price.**

The villages of Palestine

Much has changed in the last 100 years, particularly in the last few decades. About 400 Palestinian villages were physically destroyed and often their names removed from the map during the 'naqba' of 1948. Those that remain, mostly on the West Bank, retain some of their traditional houses which, built of local stone, consequently merge harmoniously with the landscape. In recent years new, less sympathetic, angular concrete buildings have been added, with a large main room and several adjacent smaller ones, usually on two floors and often with verandas. Generally the new houses stand alone whereas the traditional village house were built together or 'semi-detached'. In some cases they have replaced the traditional houses which were falling into disrepair, though the warm unstructured intimacy of the villages remains – in contrast to the more regimented Israeli settlements which visually dominate and seem at discord with the land.

Many of the walks in this guide pass through Palestinian villages, allowing you to experience both the past and the present. You will almost certainly have opportunities to visit Palestinian homes. Many of the old houses still remain in the villages along the Nativity Trail and other walks in this book. Amongst the newer buildings, you will see clusters of domed stone houses often with gardens, the better housing being higher on the hill. The uppermost villages, or 'throne villages', were home to rural landlords and exhibited the best architecture (Ras Karkar for example on the way to R17).

In all the villages there was a meeting place with a nearby guest house (*madafah*). This area was traditionally male dominated, whilst the women would meet at the spring (*ain*) as in Bethlehem (R31). There was also usually a traditional clay bread oven or *taboun*, some of which are still in use as at Yanun (R8). Additionally, there were threshing floors and oil-presses as at Lifta (R22). Houses were generally single storey, and household activities took place in courtyards, where food was cooked on a brazier or *qanun*. The better-off homes in more prosperous villages exhibit decorative masonry with upper storeys as in Lifta (R22).

Though simple in the interior, with a *mastabeh* (living room), *rawiyeh* (food storage area) and *qa' al-bayt* (stable) below for livestock, as elsewhere in the world, the traditional Palestinian home has a natural ambience frequently denied the modern house. Its form represents a symbiotic relationship between man and nature developed over hundreds, if not thousands, of years. You will find homes based on the same basic principles in the hill villages of the Himalaya and the Berber villages of Morocco, everywhere in fact where man has lived in

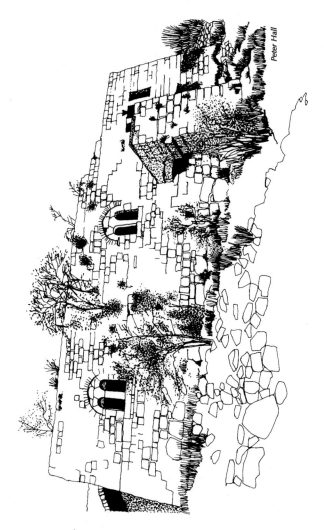

Peter Hall

A relic of the 'naqba' – one of the ruined houses in the Palestinian village of Lifta, R22

harmony with the land in a seasonal climate demanding shelter from the elements.

To appreciate the traditional village life of Palestine, you should at the very least visit the Folk and Olive Press Museums in Bethlehem (R31), or the village of Lifta (sadly evacuated in 1948, see R22) or Artas with its Folk Museum (R32). To discover what life was like in the urban centres, spend some time exploring the arched alleyways that squeeze between the old houses of the casbah in Nablus (R16) or in the maze of the Arab Quarter of Jerusalem Old City (off R20). Visit their little local shops. Experience the Hammam or Turkish Bath for which Nablus is famous, or even try the *nargileh* or 'hubble-bubble' with your coffee in a street café.

What better ways to meet the people!

Recommended reading: *The Palestinian Village Home*, Suad Amiry and Vera Tamari, British Museum Publication, 1989.

***The Mass Destruction of Palestinian Houses on the West Bank.* For this, and associated subjects, contact The Israeli Information Centre for Human Rights. Email: btselem@actcom.co.il Website: www.btselem.org**

Also contact:

RIWAQ – Center for Architectural Conservation, Ash-Sharafeh St., PO Box 212, Ramallah. Tel: 02 240 6887/6925-6, Fax: 02 240 6986, E-mail: riwaq@palnet.com, Website: www.riwaq.org

Politics and religion

'Never discuss politics and religion.'

That's the usual maxim, but in Palestine their physical presence is everywhere: Israeli settlements rise from the hills of the Occupied Territories; mosques, monasteries, churches and synagogues are part of everyday life. Soldiers, police, holy men and believers of every persuasion are omnipresent. However, you should find that everyone is polite, courteous and helpful to visitors, so if the opportunity offers itself, take part in the debate, listen to the various viewpoints, learn and contribute.

Much has changed in Palestine in recent years (see 'The Palestinians', above). Different areas of Palestine have different classifications: Zone A (about 10% of the West Bank) is mostly Palestinian city centres under full control of the Palestinian National Authority (PNA) since 1994–5.

Zone B, which covers 30% of the West Bank and is usually beyond the city check points, and is administered by the PNA whilst Israel retains control of security. Zone C, which covers the remaining 60% is mostly countryside (Palestinian agricultural land and villages, Israeli settlements and military bases) and is under total Israeli control. This means that Israel can 'close' the West Bank whenever they wish (which obviously makes life extremely difficult for Palestinians and their economy.) There are also H Zones in Hebron – where inner city settlements cause the traditional Palestinian inhabitants particular problems. Finally, the division between 'Israel' and 'Palestine' is known as the Green Line. Here again you will find checkpoints which, for the visitor, can be an inconvenience but should not be a problem.

Zones B and C are under negotiation, but the settlements and their linking 'bypass roads' that form a web across the West Bank could remain under Israeli control for the foreseeable future. This obviously further complicates life for Palestinians as they are unable to pass though them (though Israelis can go anywhere). The settlements have also greatly reduced the availability of spring water in nearby Palestinian villages.

Despite the convoluted politics and religious differences, it is highly unlikely you will meet with any harassment in Palestine; you are more likely to be overwhelmed by hospitality.

The terrain

Whilst the political boundaries could well change again if the hoped for 'just and lasting peace' is realised, give or take a few Rift Valley earthquakes, deforestation and climate changes, the geography of the land remains much as it was when early man arrived here over a million years ago. The valleys, hills, mountains, ravines and deserts explored in this guide were not only home to our ancestors, but feature throughout the Bible. The walks pass through three geographic zones.

• **The Central Uplands** Diverse in character, they include:

  The Lower Galilee Situated to the north of the Jezreel Valley with rolling fertile hills rising to 562m at Mount Tabor. This is the high, isolated hill thought to be the location of Christ's Transfiguration when he spoke with Moses and Elijah. It is visited on the first day of the Nativity Trail as well as providing a short but unique walk of its own.

  Merj ibn Amir and Nahr Jalud (Plain of Esdraelon and Valley of Jezreel) A low lying, fertile agricultural area and site of many famous biblical and historic battles, crossed on the first day of the Nativity Trail.

Jebel Nablus Located to the south of Jezreel. In the west these hills are relatively low lying with traditional terracing and olive groves, as found in Lower Galilee. R17 descends one such valley. The eastern hills are generally higher and wilder than their western and northern counterparts, rising to around 1000m south of Bethlehem, but in general, about 700–900m. They are split by wadies or ravines that plunge east to the sub-sea-level Jordan Valley. The Nativity Trail starts in the hills of Lower Galilee and crosses the Jezreel Valley, before ascending and crossing the Nablus Hills. It then descends into the Jordan Valley where the Bethlehem Wilderness starts, near Jericho.

- **The Jordan Valley** This deep cleft in the earth's crust is rich and fertile wherever there is water, but in its absence abruptly changes to arid desert. Extending from Lebanon to the Red Sea, this section of the Rift Valley commences at 200m below sea level at Galilee and descends to 400m below sea level – the lowest point on earth – at the Dead Sea. The Nativity Trail passes through here, perhaps overnighting in a Bedouin camp and also in a monastery near the Jordan River, not far from the baptismal site.

- **The Bethlehem Wilderness** This biblical wilderness reaches up from beyond the north end of the Dead Sea (at minus 400m) to the hills east of Jerusalem and Bethlehem at 700–1000m. Except where it is cut by deep ravines with their own perennial streams and linear oases, it is barren and harsh terrain, apparently unforgiving yet still home to the Bedouin. Also, because of its wadi systems such as the unique Wadi Qelt, which provides some excellent and varied treks (R12 and R23, etc), it has a surprising variety of wildlife. Many important biblical and religious sites are found here, such as the cliff-hugging monasteries of The Mount of Temptation, St George's and Mar Saba, all of which are visited by the Nativity Trail and other walks in this book.

ON THE MOVE

'Many travellers on returning home safe and sound are not content until they have published some anecdotes of how they were in danger of being attacked by robbers, or how they saw them in the distance, but kept them from coming nearer by the sight of their arms. I must be excused a little incredulity on this respect as, after travelling in all parts

of Palestine for eight years both by day and night, in good weather and in bad, in moonlight and in darkness, both alone and in company in dangerous places, I have never met with any insult.'

Customs and Traditions of Palestine, Ermette Pierotte, 1864

Where to go

This book covers the cities, towns, villages, mountains, valleys and deserts of the West Bank. The route descriptions commence with the Nativity Trail. The other routes are then described from north to south. Generally, those in the north are in a greener, kinder environment requiring the least experience – though the ascent to Faqu'a from the Jezreel Valley is not the easiest of walks! Most routes start from villages and can be reached from Jerusalem, though it may be better to stay a night in Nazareth or Nablus for quick access to walks in the north.

Moving south, there are still some short walks to be done, but the ravines that cut through the hills down to the Jordan Valley and Dead Sea offer spectacular and often unexpected scenery. They are very rewarding for those wanting real adventures, but beware of flash floods! We have also included some caves, but going beyond the initial Cathedral Chamber in the Cave of Chariton is for experienced cavers only.

Last but by no means least we have included walks in some of Palestine's ancient cities – Nablus, Jerusalem and Bethlehem. Easy walks for anyone, but fascinating and not to be missed!

When to go

'Spring is a fleeting season. Fresh from the winter rains, hills and pastures are cloaked in a lushness that passes quickly. Wild flowers burst into a riot of colour, then vanish, and the desert, momentarily brushed with tint of green from wisps of new grass, lies burnished again by a relentless sun. The sky takes on its summer tone of cloudless, pastel blue. Not a drop of rain will fall until November.'

Arab and Jew. Wounded Spirits in a Promised Land,
David K. Shipler, 1986

There are two main seasons: one starts in April and ends in October during which time the weather is hot, sunny and dry; the second begins in November and ends in March, when the weather is temperate. Average temperatures range from 9 to 18°C in winter and 26 to 30°C in summer. Highs, especially in the sub-sea-level Jordan Valley can be around 40°C.

In the midsummer month (June through to August inclusive) temperatures will be too hot for most, but otherwise the walks in this book can be enjoyed at any time of the year. Suffice it to say that there could be rain almost anywhere on the West Bank during the winter months of November to March, but particularly in the north. Winter, of course, also has short days. It could snow on the hills; it is not unusual, for example, for Jerusalem to have a fall of snow, creating a Christmas card scene. Though unlikely, it is well to remember that, if you are walking in narrow valleys or ravines, even a dry wadi may quickly flood if it rains heavily.

By late summer the land is (as David Shipler says) burnished to a golden brown, though there is not a total absence of colour. Around the villages red roses will be seen. Sweet scented white jasmine and the pretty orange, red and purple flowers of Bougainvillaea hang suspended in colourful clouds from walls and supporting trees. Bright orange flowers illuminate the greenery whilst spears of white squill, yellow groundsel and other autumn and winter flowers dot the dry wadies. By the springs and small oases, you will find oleanders in bloom, with their pink and white flowers. Fruit trees are ripe for picking. The 'festival' atmosphere at the start of the olive picking season (after the first winter rains, which are usually in late October) is worth seeing – you will no doubt be invited to join in! The delicious oranges, pomegranates and other fruits of Jericho in the Jordan Valley also ripen at this time of year.

The best seasons are undoubtedly spring and autumn, late March through to mid-May, and late September to mid-November. April is undoubtedly our favourite month: the winter rains should have finished, streams are flowing and the land – especially in the north – is green and carpeted with flowers. If you are lucky you will even see pockets of colour in the desert hills to the south. At this time of year, wandering the hills and valleys is a real pleasure, and you may well discover your own walks in this generally gentle terrain.

However, if you are on a pilgrimage you may have other reasons to choose the time of your visit, such as the celebrations of Christmas or Easter, but remember the towns and cities will be busy and hotels may well be full, so book early. (Also see 'Holidays and holy days', below.)

Travel tips

There are numerous Middle East guidebooks with advice on international travel (see 'Relevant books and websites' in Appendices). For a hassle-free journey, many people advise travelling via Jordan. Suffice it

Peter Hall

The Damascus Gate, Jerusalem

to say that British Air now fly to Jordan from London, whilst other airlines fly from Manchester to Jordan via major European cities. Royal Jordanian Airlines fly daily from London, Paris and many European cities to Amman. Their UK address is:

Royal Jordanian Airlines, 32 Brook Street, London. WIY 1AG.

Tel: 0171 878 6333, Fax: 0171 629 4069

Dependent on route and airline, return fares from Europe vary between £200 and £450 (about $270–$600). Cheaper prices generally imply less comfort and longer times. Take the most convenient way and you can be in Jordan from the UK in 5 hours and in Palestine the next morning. A cheaper option may well take double that. Such is life!

For British travellers, tourist information on Jordan is available from:

The Jordan Tourist Board,
Unit 1 Blades Court,
121 Deodar Rd, London SW15 2NU. Tel: 0181 877 0554.

For information on Palestine contact:

Palestine National Authority, Ministry of Tourism and Antiquities
PO Box 534, Bethlehem, Palestine
Tel: 00972 2 2741581, Fax: 00972 2 2743753
E-mail: mota@visit-palestine.com, Website: www.visit-palestine.com

British citizens in Palestine may wish to register at the
British Consulate-General in Jerusalem. Tel: 00972 2 541 4100.

Palestinian info for British citizens: www.britishconsulate.org

General world travel info for British citizens: www.fco.gov.uk/travel/

UK Travellers could also contact any of the following for individual or group travel:

Freelance Travel Ltd, 6 Church Street, Twyford, Reading, Berks RG10 9ED. Tel: 01189 320 311; out of office hours: 01189 341 398;
Fax: 01189 342 681(24hrs)
E-mail: freelancetravel@btconnect.com

The Imaginative Traveller, 14 Barley Mow Passage, Chiswick, London W4 4PH. Tel: 0181 742 3113, Fax: 0181 742 3045
Arabica Travel Ltd, PO Box 26119, London SW8 4RZ
Tel: 0171 640 2332, Fax: 0171 627 3748
E-mail: arabica@annal.dircon.co.uk

For trekking holidays in Palestine, contact:
Alternative Tourism Group, PO Box 173, Beit Sahour, Palestine
Tel: 02 277 2151, Fax: 02 277 2211
E-mail: atg@p-ol.com, Website: www.patg.org

Guiding Star Ltd, Virgin Mary Street, Beit Jala, PO Box 1161,
Bethlehem, Palestine
Tel: 02 276 5970, Fax: 02 276 5971
E-mail: info@guidingstar2.com Website: www.GuidingStarLtd.com

Money matters

If you are passing through Jordan the unit of currency is the Jordanian
Dinar (JD). In October 2000, 1JD was worth £1.05 sterling (0.7JD/$1).
Money can be changed at money exchange offices and most banks
and larger hotels. Check around: prices do vary a little and if you're
changing a lot it can be worthwhile. (The airport exchange rate is not
the best.)

In touristic parts of Palestine, there are at least three currencies that
can be used. Visitors can ask for prices and invoices in US dollars,
Jordanian dinars, and New Israeli shekels (NIS). Foreign currencies are
widely accepted, as well as travellers' cheques and all major credit
cards. You can change money in banks, most hotels, and authorised at
money changers, where you should get the best rates. The unit of
currency in common use in Palestine is the New Israeli Shekel. In Jan
2001 it was fluctuating between 5.2 and 5.5NIS / £1 (4.1NIS / $1).

Wherever you travel in the Middle East, make sure you have some
small currency, including coins, everywhere outside major cities as
change always seems to be in short supply. Credit Cards are increasingly acceptable, but mostly confined to the larger international hotels,
shops and restaurants, or businesses dealing with tourists on a regular
basis.

Airports

The only Palestinian airport is Gaza International (Tel: 07 213 5696).
Airports conveniently situated for travel to Palestine are Ben Gurion
International (Tel: 03 972 3344) between Jerusalem and Tel Aviv in
Israel, and Queen Alia International Airport in Jordan (Tel: 009626
4453200). Due to time-consuming and sometimes humiliating security
checks at Ben Gurion, many non-Israelis prefer to enter from Jordan.

Visas

There are no medical requirements for entry to Jordan, Israel or
Palestine from most countries. Visitors to Palestine need only a valid
passport. Israeli authorities, however, require visitors to fill out an entry
visa card. Citizens of the UK, USA, Australia, New Zealand and the EU
don't need a visa beforehand. They can be obtained at border crossings

or at the Israeli airport upon arrival. If you pass through Israel and intend travelling elsewhere in the Middle East it is advisable to get your visa stamped onto your entry card rather than into your passport. The one good thing about all this is that it's free; the snag is, that you have to pay 118NIS to get back through the Israeli border!

Visas for Jordan can be obtained beforehand from the Jordanian Embassy (visa info, tel: 0891 117 1261). The UK address is: 6 Upper Phillimore Gardens, London W8 7HB.

You can also get your Jordanian visa at the airport and most other entry points to Jordan. They currently cost 10JD regardless of nationality and are valid for fourteen days. If your visit to Jordan and Palestine will be longer than this, you will need to get a visa extension before leaving Jordan. This is simply and freely obtained in Amman from the nearest Police Station to where you are staying. Your hotel may do it for you. Otherwise ask a taxi driver to take you (there is one downtown, one at the 3rd Circle and one at the 8th Circle). If you are in south Jordan there is a Police Station in Aqaba (opposite the bus station). The visa extension will be added whilst you wait and shouldn't take more than ten minutes, but beware of being caught out by holidays.

Crossing from Jordan to Israel (and vice versa) remember that an Israeli stamp or even a Jordanian or Egyptian stamp from an Israeli border crossing point may preclude entry to countries such as Syria and Lebanon. Ask them not to stamp your passport.

Transport in Jordan

The costs and availability of public transport in Jordan are covered in general travel books such as Lonely Planet's *Jordan and Syria, A Travel Survival Kit.* From Amman's Queen Alia Airport, there are regular JETT (Jordan Express Tourist Transport) bus services to Abdali Bus Station in Amman leaving every 30–40 minutes from 6.00–22.00 and every two hours through the night. The cost is 1JD plus 0.25JD for bags. Or, of course, you can take a taxi.

For Palestine, the most commonly used border crossing between Amman, in north Jordan, and Jerusalem is the King Hussein Bridge (referred to as the Allenby Bridge in Israel), though from further north there is also a crossing point at the Sheikh Hussein Bridge. In the south you can cross from Aqaba to Eilat in Israel.

There are JETT buses from Abdali bus station down to the King Hussein Bridge. Other buses and service-taxis also leave from Abdali from 6.00 onwards. It's 1JD for the bus and 1.5JD for the taxi (about

12 to 15JD in a private taxi). The journey takes about one hour. Allow another hour to cross the border (1.5JD for the bus over the bridge) and one more to reach Jerusalem (30NIS by service taxi).

Transport in Palestine

The easiest means of transportation in Palestine are the frequent buses and share-taxis ('taxi service' or simply 'servis'). These are large cars or small vans that drive along main routes and stop anywhere upon request. They usually depart from places such as the Damascus Gate (Bab el Amud) in Jerusalem, Mujam'aa car park near Manara Square in Ramallah, Bab S'qaq in Bethlehem, and in city centres generally. They are reasonably cheap (3NIS from East Jerusalem to Bethlehem for example – a distance of 10km – for exchange rates see 'Money matters', above). Private or 'special taxis' are a useful and sometimes necessary alternative but they do not always have meters, so you should negotiate the price in advance. They are much more expensive than the servis: a typical cost for the above journey would be 35NIS and maybe 100NIS from Jerusalem to Nablus. Negotiate and agree the price first!

Accommodation

Accommodation in Palestine varies from simple hostels at about 15 NIS/person up to first-class international hotels at whatever price you can afford. See the usual travel guides for information.

Accommodation along the Nativity Trail varies from village homes and community centres to Bedouin camps and monasteries. It will be booked for you if your trek is organised by a Palestinian agent (for example Alternative Travel Group or Guiding Star). If you wish to make your own arrangements, details are given at the end of each day's route description, together with contacts, taxis, nearest hospitals, etc. It is also possible to camp, though when close to, or within view of, a village it would be polite to ask first and sensible to enquire about the availability of water and toilet facilities.

For hotels in Palestine, contact:

The Arab Hotel Association, PO Box 66206, Jerusalem.

Tel: 02 6281805, Website: www.palestinehotels.com

VISITING AND WALKING INFORMATION

Time

Palestine is situated in +2.00 GMT Time Zone (+3.00 GMT in summer). This, by the way, can be a bit confusing at the times when the clocks change: Palestine changes with Jordan, but this is about a week before

Israel changes, so for that week you need to be sure whose time zone you are in – it could well be both!

Working hours are generally 8.00–19.00. Palestinian government offices generally open 8.00–14.30. Banks open 8.00–12.30 (some also open 15.00–17.00). The official holiday is on Friday, but some shops close on Sundays.

Holidays and holy days

This being the Holy Land, there is a profusion of holidays; some are fixed dates, others vary. Islamic and Jewish dates depend on the first sighting of the new moon and therefore move back by about 11 days annually. The different religious and national holidays are, of course, only celebrated by the relevant communities. You should, however, be particularly aware of Ramadan when Muslims fast from sunrise to sunset for 28 days. This, and other Muslim holidays, affects the whole of the West Bank (Palestine) and its borders. Jewish holidays do not affect Palestine but affect borders and flights. Christian holidays mostly take place in Jerusalem, Bethlehem and parts of Ramallah and Nazareth. Armenian holidays are only celebrated by their own community.

Muslim holidays — 2002

Eid Al-Adha	23–25 February
Al-Hejira	13 March
Moulid Al-Nabi	23 May
Start of Ramadan	5 November
Eid Al-Fitr (End of Ramadan)	3 December

Jewish and Israeli holidays

Passover	28 March
Shevuot	17 May
New Year	7 September
Yom Kippur	16 September
Succoth	21 September
Simhat Torah	28 September

Christian holidays

Easter	between late March and late April
Christmas Day	25 December
New Year	1 January
Orthodox Christmas	7 January
Orthodox New Year	13 January

Palestinian holidays

Fatah Day	1 January
Independence Day	15 November

Communication breakdown

Palestinians, of course, speak Arabic, but English is the second language and many speak it fluently. Most have at least enough English to offer advice and have a simple conversation. However, you should try to speak a few words of Arabic – it always helps. Have a try, the worst you can do is make someone smile! Most travel guides have a section with key words and phrases or you can get pocket guides to Arabic such as Berlitz or Penguin or the BBC Language series supported by tapes. (Also see 'Useful Arabic/English words' in the Appendix of this book.)

The weekly English newspaper is the *Jerusalem Times*. For international news and the Israeli viewpoint see the *Herald Tribune/Haaretz*, which is widely available in Palestinian towns; also, the leading European and American papers can be bought in the international hotels. Radio Jordan (in English) with news, interviews, weather forecasts and a variety of music is broadcast on FM 96.3–99 MHz. Jordan TV also has quite a lot of English and French programmes, whilst satellite TV with programmes such as CNN News can be seen in the larger hotels and at many households. If you get withdrawal symptoms away from a computer, there are plenty of Internet Cafés.

Public phones in Palestine work either with coins or phone cards. Phone cards are available at the Palestinian post offices. The international code for Israel is 972. This also works for Palestine, but the correct code for Palestine is 970. When calling from Jordan you need to call 970. To call overseas, you must dial 00 (or 012, 013,014 if you're in Jerusalem). For information, call 144.

The postal service is reliable but you should not use Palestinian stamps in Israel or vice versa – a complicated world, isn't it!

Food and drink

For lightweight provisions (dehydrated foods), as well as fresh foods, the major towns generally have a good selection. The smaller villages have less choice, but you can usually find bread, vegetables, powdered milk, tinned fish and other foods, biscuits, tea, coffee, sugar and bottled water. A vegetarian diet is the cheapest! The best place to shop for fresh fruit and veg is always in the local markets. In the smallest villages, there may be no shops at all, so be sure you have enough provisions with you if you are trekking for a few days.

The larger towns also have a good choice of restaurants and cafés of all standards serving international or local Arabic foods, with a range of prices to match. The more expensive ones are also likely to sell alcoholic drinks. Many of the smaller villages also have at least one street café for locals, which are always friendly places to eat in as well as inexpensive. Eating out in Palestine will cost you less than in Israel or in most parts of Europe. If you eat in street cafés and buy local Palestinian produce for your treks, it will cost you far less.

Remember that during Ramadan most food shops and cafés are closed during daylight hours; smoking is frowned upon and alcoholic drinks are banned at this time except in some international restaurants and non-Muslim areas.

Clothing and equipment

'The traveller should take with him a plaid, an overcoat, and a suit for visiting consuls, attending divine service etc., but dress clothes are quite unnecessary. The tailor should be instructed to make the sewing extra strong, for repairs and sewing buttons on are dear in the East, not to speak of the difficulty of finding the tailor just when he is wanted.'

Palestine and Syria,
Karl Baedeke, Leipzig, 1898

Palestine can be cold at night, especially in the north or on the hills (it may even snow in mid-winter!), so have some warm and preferably windproof clothes. Waterproofs can be useful in the north in winter and the occasional storm can be very severe, causing flash floods. Conversely the lack of water can be an ever-present problem. If you are returning to base at night, and it's not too hot, then you can manage on 1–2 litres a day. On long, hot and strenuous days you should allow for 1 litre of water per hour – certainly a minimum of 5 litres of water/day. If you are camping, a minimum of 4–5 litres a day is essential whatever the temperature. If you expect to get water from wells you may need to carry 6–7m of strong, thin cord (and remember to ask permission).

Peter Hall

Wooden pestles and mortars

Except in mid-winter, lightweight clothing, with a fleece jacket, windproof top, sunglasses and sun hat will be adequate for most routes. Shorts are fine up on the mountains, weather permitting, though on a hot day you may suffer sunburn and will lose precious body moisture quickly and without noticing, leading to speedy dehydration. Whatever you wear remember to dress with respect for any holy places you may be visiting; also, respect local traditions if you want to be welcomed into Bedouin camps or the houses of local people.

Trainers or modern lightweight trekking boots are all that's needed for footwear; even modern 'trekking sandals' can be worn on easier walks, but you could regret it if you disturb a scorpion or, worse still, a snake! (Although we've seen plenty of snakes in the Middle East including Palestinian Vipers and the much more venomous Horned Viper, we've never heard of anyone being bitten – see 'Be prepared', below.)

You should, of course, have your own first aid kit, a multi-blade knife and head torch with spare batteries. If you intend camping, take the lightest possible sleeping bag, tent, etc, and a Gaz or multi-fuel stove. If you are staying near a village or Bedouin camp the residents may be able to arrange food for you. (Information is given at the end of some route descriptions.) As always you should have a compass and the relevant maps with you to supplement the maps in this book, though a guide with knowledge of the area is always worth having and usually good company.

Taking a guide

Many visitors to Palestine are experienced enough to do any of the routes in this book without guides. Others come with qualified trekking guides to lead their party. Nevertheless, using the facilities of a Palestinian agency or local guide with knowledge of the area is always worthwhile, and will not only provide you with in-depth knowledge of the land and people, but also guarantee access to local communities. Additionally, on multi-day treks such as the Nativity Trail, the complex logistics of travel and accommodation are solved. This enables you to trek with minimal gear (just enough for one day), allowing you maximum enjoyment of the walk and the Palestinian hospitality arranged for you at your next overnight stop!

Palestinian agents familiar with the Nativity Trail are Alternative Tourism Group and Guiding Star. See 'Community tourism', above, for full details.

Maps

The current 1:50,000 maps which include Palestine are the 'Hiking and Touring' Maps published by the Society for the Protection of Nature in Israel (SPNI) and the Survey of Israel Series. The relevant map numbers are given at the beginning of each route with the suffix SPNI for the former and SOIS for the latter. Grid references are eight figure and refer to the black grid numbers. All maps are available from the SPNI Office in Jerusalem, at: 13 Heleni Hamalka St, PO Box 930, Jerusalem 91008, Tel: 02 624 4605 / 625 2357.

Other places such as bookshops and hotels sell general maps which include Palestine, such as the 1:100,000 road maps of Israel, whilst most travel guidebooks have some road and town maps. For a good selection of books and maps, walk up Salah ed Din St, just east of Jerusalem's Damascus Gate and opposite Herod's (Zahra) Gate, to visit the Educational Bookshop and the American Colony Hotel Bookshop (0.5 and 1km respectively). You could also contact specialist map suppliers in Europe.

The following maps are all useful:

The Times Concise Atlas of the Bible, Times Books 1991

Palestine – The Holy Land Tourist Map, Palestinian Ministry of Tourism and Antiquities, Bethlehem

Map of Jerusalem and Bethlehem, Arab Hotel Association (free from hotels)

Israel, 1:250,000 northern sheet,1997

The maps in this book were made by the authors. Apart from the few city maps and the cave survey, all other maps are based on originals supplied by:

Applied Research Institute – Jerusalem (ARIJ)
Caritas Street, PO Box 860, Bethlehem, Palestine
Tel: 02 274 1889, Fax: 02 277 6966
E-mail: postmaster@arij.org,
Website: www.arij.org

The combination of the maps and route descriptions in this book should be adequate to find all the routes and also

KEY TO TREKKING MAPS IN THIS BOOK	
▨	Palestinian town or village
▨	Israeli settlement
▨	Sea or lake
▬▬▬	Major road
─────	Minor road or track
··········	Walk / trek
‒ ‒ ‒ ‒	Wadi (permanent or seasonal stream or river)
	Contour (100m intervals)

to follow some, though route-finding skills will be needed for the more complex treks due to the inevitably small scale of the maps and consequent limited information. It is always advisable to supplement them with the relevant 1:50,000 maps.

Be prepared!

Some routes are easy strolls taking only an hour or so. Others are more serious undertakings, sometimes crossing complex terrain with no water sources and always with inadequate maps when compared to the large-scale European ones. On top of that, there are sometimes only disconnected shepherds' paths or even none at all! Furthermore, it's likely to be hot and, because of the water situation and the amount of gear you may have with you, you may well be carrying more than 10 kilos. On long, hot and strenuous days, when you want to carry the least, you will need a minimum of 5 litres of water per person – that's 5 kilos, before you add other essentials – such is life!

You also need to be self-sufficient as, on some of the routes in this guide, the only people you may meet are Bedouin shepherds. If you have an accident or get lost it will be up to you to extricate yourself. As always, what you carry will be a compromise between weight, comfort and safety. Your pack should always include a first aid kit and other items such as water purifiers and sun creams, etc (see 'Clothing and equipment', above).

Be aware that as well as mosquitoes, which can sometimes be a nuisance, it is also possible (despite tents with mosquito nets) to be bitten by minute sand flies which may carry *Leishmaniesis*. The result is unsightly scabs, which appear three or four months later and take another eight months or so to disappear, possibly leaving a small scar. To avoid sand flies it is always best to sleep away from water and vegetation. It is, apparently, also possible to get malaria; we have never taken any anti-malaria tablets, but insect repellent creams are probably a wise precaution if sleeping out near wadies and pools. Cases of mosquito-carried Nile Fever have recently also been reported in the Jordan Valley.

Snake bites and scorpion stings are almost unheard of, but be careful in thick vegetation which may conceal either, and avoid picking up stones (for example to clear a campsite) as scorpions may be hiding there during the heat of the day. If bitten or stung, try not to panic: it increases heart rate and blood flow. Nevertheless, you should get to the nearest doctor or hospital as soon as possible. (If you have a mobile phone with you, consider requesting an ambulance to meet you – see below.) Scorpion bites are rarely fatal to adults, though they can make you ill for a few days. A bite from a viper, though extremely unlikely, is usually much more venomous and should be taken seriously.

There are probably only two other hazards that could seriously threaten a walk in the wilderness. First of all, flash floods – avoid narrow valleys and rocky gorges if rain is possible anywhere in the locality. If in doubt, phone the weather-line (see below). Secondly, political unrest – keep in touch with your Embassy or Consulate for information and advice on the latest events. You may well find that things are not as bad as they are portrayed in the media!

Finally, always let someone know not only where you're going, but when you expect to be back. Having made this commitment, don't go somewhere else, and do check in on your return!

Ambulance and police
The following are some useful numbers:

All areas ambulance 101

City	Ambulance	Police
Jerusalem	101	100
Nazareth	101	100
Jenin	101 / 06-2503537	06-2501035
Nablus	101 / 09-2385077	09-2383518
Ramallah	101 / 02-2957574	02-2956571
Jericho	101 / 02-2957574	02-2322521
Bethlehem	101 / 02-2743225	02-2748231
Hebron	101 / 02-2228598	02-2228598

Tourism and antiquities police
Bethlehem	02-2770750/1
Jericho	02-2324011
Nablus	09-385244

Telephone services
Information	144
Weather	03-9668855

Border crossings
Allenby Bridge	02-9943358

As mobile phones now work in most parts of Palestine outside the deeper mountain valleys and canyons leading down to the Rift Valley, it is now possible to phone directly for help in emergency. Please don't abuse the system.

OTHER OUTDOOR ACTIVITIES

Rock climbing

The rock climbing in the West Bank, which is generally on excellent and usually steep limestone crags, has mostly been developed by Israeli climbers. The few cliffs that have established routes tend have fixed gear (for example in Wadi Qelt). Climbing access agreements in Nature Reserves/International Birdlife Areas should be respected.

For details, contact:

Israeli Alpine Club, PO Box 39101, Jerusalem 91390
Tel: 02 6236551, E-mail: relkatz@yahoo.com

Caving

'When planning a caving trip think of the return journey and remember that caving grades only apply to fit, competent and properly equipped parties; novices in particular will find caves harder than indicated and for most systems there must be sufficient and competent cavers in the party.'

Advice from a British caving guide

The caves in this guide include the most extensive in Palestine – the Cave of Chariton – which has 3450m of passages (R35). There are many caves in this part of the world, some of which await further exploration. Caving is a serious business for experienced people only. An 'active-cave' – that is, one which has (or could have) water running through it – will be subject to flood hazard. If in doubt, don't!

For further information on caves in Palestine, contact:

Israeli Cave Research Centre, Tel: 02 976740 or 976411.
Cave Research Section, Hebrew University of Jerusalem,
Tel: 02 9975541, Fax: 02 820549

Route descriptions

Each route description in this guide details its special features, interests and risks, the grade of difficulty, distance covered with altitude changes and the time required for an average party. The time given may seem a lot for the distance, but trekking in the Middle East is much more demanding than in more temperate climates, so don't expect to cover the same amount of ground, even if it is virtually all downhill! Minor errors in route finding can lose considerable time; heat and dehydration are your greatest enemies.

The approach is also described, before giving details of the route, followed by, if necessary, the return and any useful information on transport and accommodation. The terms 'true left' and 'true right' apply when looking down a mountain, canyon, wadi or valley, whereas directions to go 'left' or 'right' apply to the direction of travel, whether in ascent or descent, and are abbreviated to L and R. Compass points are abbreviated to N S E W, for north, south, etc, whilst route numbers in the text and on the maps are prefixed by R. Distances and heights are in metric, as is altitude (abbreviated to alt.). They are quoted in kilometres (km) or metres (m). Four-wheel drive is abbreviated to 4wd, and times in hours and minutes are shown as hrs and mins.

Apart from three walks, the routes in this guide have all been done by the authors. The descriptions of the three not checked by us are based on notes supplied by others, and the words 'Not verified by the authors' appear in the route introduction. Finally, although we walked the Nativity Trail in spring 2000 we were not asked to write this book until later. Despite our best intentions, events in October 2000 prevented us from re-checking all but a couple of days of the trail. Those descriptions are therefore partially based on notes by the trail's creators.

Anyone doing any routes in this book and having useful comments to make, or anyone with details of new routes, should send their notes for inclusion in future editions of this guide to either:

Cicerone Press, 2 Police Square, Milnthorpe, Cumbria, LA7 7PY England or

n.o.m.a.d.s. Greenman's Farm, Greenfield, Oldham, OL3 7HA England

Grading of walks and treks

There is, as yet, no internationally agreed grading system for treks. As a consequence, the grades below are specific to the routes in this guide; they bear no correlation to the grades in our guide *Jordan – Walks, Treks, Caves, Climbs and Canyons*, nor to those in other guidebooks.

- **Easy walk** Usually short, with no difficulties such as scrambling on rock or scree, no exposure to heights, no unduly arduous ascents or descents and no serious route-finding problems.

- **Moderate trek** Usually half to one day. Altitude differences may be considerable. Some easy scrambling may be necessary and experience in route finding could be required.

- **Serious trek** Amongst the longest in this guide, these routes pass through the more remote areas and require stamina, self-sufficiency and confidence in rocky terrain. There could be considerable ascent and/or descent and route-finding experience is essential.

Grading of rock scrambles

A few treks include rock scrambles. This is noted both in the route introduction as well as in the actual description and shown in brackets, for example (Grade 2).

- **Grade 1** The point at which hands are required for balance or safety.
- **Grade 2** Generally steeper rock, but with good holds for security.

Grading of caves

- **Easy cave. Grade 1** No rope-work or technical difficulties. Route finding may present problems for the uninitiated.
- **Moderate cave. Grade 2** This grade includes small pot-holes. Ropes may be required for ascent and descent. Possibly quite long. Some experience necessary.
- **Serious Cave. Grade 3 or more** Definitely experienced cavers only.

Old Jerusalem

Peter Hall

Do not attempt any other than
the 'Easy' routes in this book
without either adequate experience or a guide.

THE NATIVITY TRAIL

R1 Introduction

The Year 2000 Journey from Nazareth (City of the Annunciation) to Bethlehem (City of the Nativity)

'The Nativity Trail winds 160 kilometres through the hills and villages of Palestine. It was opened in the millennium year to celebrate the birth of Christ, and to enable trekkers to enjoy the country whilst learning about the land and its people. It is a part of the Bethlehem 2000 Project, 'to encourage tourists and pilgrims ... and to enhance the economical development of Palestine as a crucial part of building peace'. As a Palestinian friend said, "It is more than just a trek, it is a pilgrimage for social justice" which was something we came to appreciate as the journey unfolded.'

'The Nativity Trail', Tony Howard,
Adventure Travel Magazine, Sept 2000

Serious trek: 140–210km. The usual route is about 150–160km and is normally walked in 10 days. Alternatively, any of the days may be enjoyed as a single day's hike or combined to make short treks. Mostly 'Easy' to 'Moderate' with one 'Serious' day.

Special interest Walking the Nativity Trail is an opportunity to experience the full range of the Palestinian landscape, from the green hills of the north to the desert of the south. You will also meet a diverse range of people: Franciscan priests on Mount Tabor, Muslim clerics at the village mosques, Greek Orthodox monks in desert monasteries, hillside farmers and their families, small-town shopkeepers and craftspeople, Bedouin shepherds and many others. In the predominantly agricultural area, you will encounter men, women and children engaged in ploughing fields, winnowing wheat and picking olives according to the season. On the hills you will meet Bedouin watering their flocks at ancient cisterns.

Everywhere you will be greeted with 'Ahlan Wasahlan' – a warm welcome and traditional gesture of hospitality. You may be treated to a cup of sweet tea, some freshly baked *taboun* bread, or even a friendly game of billiards in the village 'club' – and always, delicious Palestinian cuisine!

For twenty centuries, people have been telling the Christmas story about the birth of Jesus in Bethlehem. People of all faiths can identify with the young mother-to-be, Mary, travelling by donkey with her husband, Joseph, all the way from the village of Nazareth in Galilee to the distant town of Bethlehem – a journey of many long days and nights. Why did they make such a trek? The young couple were required by the Roman tax collectors to register in the city of Bethlehem. It is one of the most famous passages in the Bible:

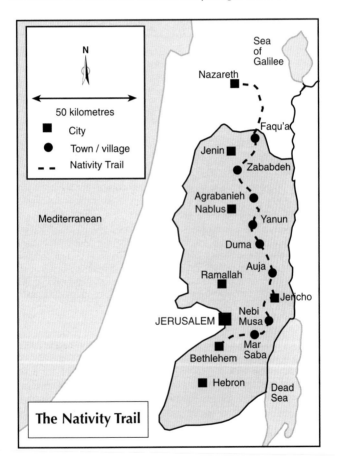

The Nativity Trail

'In those days Caesar Augustus issued a decree that a census should be taken of the entire Roman world. (This was the first census that took place while Quirinius was governor of Syria.) And everyone went to his own town to register. So Joseph also went up from the town of Nazareth in Galilee to Judea, to Bethlehem the town of David, because he belonged to the house and line of David. He went there to register with Mary, who was pledged to be married to him and was expecting a child. While they were there, the time came for the baby to be born, and she gave birth to her firstborn, a son. She wrapped him in cloths and placed him in a manger, because there was no room for them in the inn.'

Luke 2: 1-7, *Holy Bible, NIV*

Now, 2000 years later, the Bethlehem 2000 Project invites you to make a symbolic and historic journey commemorating that event by walking Palestine's Nativity Trail. This carefully researched route is the first leg of a new Palestinian Trail being developed for the Year 2000 and beyond. Inaugurated for the celebration of the millennium, you can be among the first to participate.

Where to stay? On treks arranged with a Palestine Travel Agent, hikers will stay in villagers' homes or local community centres, experiencing the legendary hospitality of Palestinians. Other nights, accommodation will be in monasteries or Bedouin tents, or at campsites where hikers can pitch their own tents or sleep under the stars. They will need to provide their own sleeping bags and mattresses, tent, water bottles, etc. Those trekking independently will need to make their own arrangements well in advance for food and accommodation, or to carry camping equipment and sufficient food for 2 to 3 days at all times.

What kind of terrain does the trail cover? Just like travellers in biblical times, hikers will be traversing varied terrain: agricultural valleys, olive groves, forested or sometimes steep hills in the north and rougher terrain to the south, with rocky hillsides and gorges, sub-sea-level desert and barren uplands.

Who can participate? This is an outdoor adventure for the physically fit with an interest in nature, history, culture and religious tradition. Participants should be able to spend 6–9hrs a day on the trail.

Guides? Organised treks led by professional guides are based on the following itinerary. (For full details, see the relevant route description.)

THE ROUTE

R2 Day 1, morning: Ascend Mount Tabor. 1.5km

After a tour of Nazareth including the Church of the Annunciation and the House of Mary, drive to the foot of Mount Tabor. Ascend Tabor and visit the Monastery of the Transfiguration. Continue by vehicle across the Jezreel Valley and then:

R3 Day 1, afternoon: Ascend from Jezreel to Faqu'a. 6–9km

A steep scramble up the Hills of Gilboa. Overnight: village accommodation (basic).

Alternatively (but seldom done and not recommended) Faqu'a can be reached on foot from Nazareth in 2–3 days:

R4 Day 1: Nazareth to Mount Tabor. 16km

After the tour of Nazareth, walk to and up Mount Tabor. Visit the Monastery. Overnight: The Monastery of the Transfiguration Guest House (closed in winter) or camping.

R5 Day 2 and 3: Mount Tabor to Taibeh and on to Faqu'a. 43km

A long day of hiking through Marj Bin Amer (Jezreel Valley), the fertile breadbasket of the region, arriving in the village of Taibeh (no overnight facilities). The journey continues across the plains of the Marj to climb Jabal Faqu'a (Mount Gilboa), with splendid views of the valley below. Overnight: village accommodation (basic).

Either way, you are now in Faqu'a, and no doubt ready for the next day. If you took the usual start, this will be your second day:

R6 Day 2: Faqu'a to Zababdeh. 20km

Across the rolling Eastern Hills of Palestine, through the villages of Jalbun and Mughayir to Zababdeh, a Christian town on the ancient Roman trade route. Overnight: accommodation in community centre (modern facilities).

R7 Day 3: Zababdeh to Aqrabanieh. 21km

Through olive groves and forests on the fertile hills of the West Bank, descending to the spring of Ain Fara'a (biblical Tirzah). Relax at the café and swim in the pool before continuing through the orange groves to the broad sweep of Wadi Bidan, a picturesque valley system rich in mountain springs. Overnight: orange grove camping or house with shower.

R8 Day 4: Aqrabanieh to Yanun. 15km

A steep morning ascent from Wadi Bidan to the pass on the E shoulder of Jebel Kabir, then a leisurely ramble past the village of Beit Dajan. A second long climb follows, then down to the isolated village of Yanun, nestled among the hills. Overnight: camping (very basic).

R9 Day 5: Yanun to Duma. 12km

The trail follows the escarpment separating the fertile highlands from the arid slopes of the Jordan Valley, offering the first views of the desert and Jordan before reaching the agricultural hilltop town of Duma with its olive groves. Overnight: village accommodation with families. (Opportunity to visit Nablus and to experience its famous Hammam or Turkish Baths – see R16.)

R10 Day 6: Duma to Ain Auja. 18km

Across deep valleys and over high hills inhabited by shepherds before descending a rocky gorge to sea level at Auja Spring, one of the largest water sources in the Jordan Valley. Overnight: camping with Bedouin shepherds near Al Auja (very basic).

R11 Day 7: Auja to Jericho. 13km

Desert terrain gives way to orange groves as the journey continues to the Mount of Temptation with its Orthodox monastery clinging to the cliffs, then to Jericho, 'the oldest city on Earth'. Overnight: orange grove camping or hotel in Jericho, or the Monastery of St Gerasimus. (Opportunity to visit the Dead Sea for a swim.)

R12 Day 8: Jericho to Nebi Musa. 14km

Up the spectacular canyon of Wadi Qelt to St George Koziba Monastery, then over the arid mountains of the Bethlehem Wilderness to the remote and dramatically situated Nebi Musa (a Muslim pilgrim site associated with Moses). Overnight: Nebi Musa guest house or camping.

R13 Day 9: Nebi Musa to Mar Saba. 8km (or 20km from Nebi Musa)

The original Nativity Trail from Nebi Musa involved walking along the road, then taking tracks directly through the desert to the legendary Orthodox monastery of Mar Saba in its wild canyon setting. The preferred route is now to drive the road, then follow desert tracks via Hyrcania, one of Herod's mountain-top fortresses. Much more interesting! Overnight: Camping outside the monastery, or with local Bedouin (very basic).

Peter Hall

The start of the Nativity Trail – Nazareth and the Church of the Annunciation

R14 Day 10: Mar Saba to Bethlehem. 9km (or 15km if you walk all the way to Bethlehem)

The trail's final segment ascends the hills of the Bethlehem Wilderness to the hilltop suburbs of Bethlehem. The way then descends on foot or by vehicle through Beit Sahour (the Shepherds' Field) to Manger Square in Bethlehem and the Church of the Nativity on the site where the original journey ended – and the Christian faith has its beginnings.

Enquiries via your travel agent, or contact:

Bethlehem 2000 – details in Preface

Alternative Travel Group – details in Introduction, Community tourism

Guiding Star Ltd – details in Introduction, Community tourism

Check out the Birzeit University website for in-depth information on the trail and nearby towns and villages: www.birzeit.edu/nz2bl/trail

The Nativity Trail starts (of course!) in the ancient Palestinian town of:

NAZARETH

'You cannot see from Nazareth the surrounding country, for Nazareth rests in a basin among hills; but the moment you climb to the edge of this basin, which is everywhere within the limit of the village boys' playground, what a view you have! Esdraelon lies before you, with its twenty battle-fields – the scenes of Barak's and Gideon's victories, the scenes of Saul's and Josiah's defeats, the scenes of the struggles for freedom in the glorious days of the Maccabees. There is Naboth's vineyards and a place of Jehu's revenge upon Jezebel; there Shunem and the house of Elisha; there Carmel and the place of Elijah's sacrifice. To the east the valley of Jordan, with the long range of Gilead; to the west the radiance of the Great Sea, with the ships of Tarshish and the promise of the Isles. You see thirty miles in three directions. It is a map of Old Testament history...'

The Historical Geography of the Holy Land, George Adam Smith, 1894

Nazareth is one of the holiest towns in Christendom, ranking next to Jerusalem and Bethlehem in its wealth of tradition, its new and ancient churches, monasteries and other religious institutions. Today Nazareth is the largest Arab town in the Galilee, and provides administrative and commercial services for the surrounding villages. The ancient centre of Nazareth, where the market and main churches are located, is still notable for its small old houses and winding alleys.

Nazareth has been occupied since the Bronze Age (Middle Canaanite Period) and according to the scriptures, it was here that Jesus spent his childhood. Here, the Annunciation of Mary took place, and it was from their home in Nazareth that Mary and Joseph travelled to Bethlehem, where Jesus was born, for a Roman census. Once his ministry began, Jesus moved to Capernaum, by the Sea of Galilee, but he returned to Nazareth on a number of occasions. When he returned to preach in the Synagogue in Nazareth, Jesus was well known, but his claim to be fulfilling the words of the prophets, and his anger at the people's lack of faith, was met with opposition, and he was thrown out of the town. Today, Nazareth is a large Arab town with a roughly equal population of Christians and Muslims. A large Jewish town, Nazareth Illit, has been built on the hills above.

Below the Nazareth Hospital is the recently discovered and renovated Early Roman Period 'Nazareth Village', a multi-faith project uniting Christians, Muslims and Jews in 'recapturing the common heritage coming from the settings at the beginning of Jesus' life and his ministry'. For information, contact:

www.mbm.org/resources/missionsnow

Accommodation St Margaret's Guest House, tel: 06 6573507 fax: 06 6567166

Some biblical references

Annunciation of Mary	Luke 1: 26–31
Mary and Joseph's journey from Nazareth to Bethlehem	Luke 2: 1–5
Childhood of Jesus	Luke 2: 39–40 and 51–52
Jesus moves to Capernaum	Mathew 2: 23; 4: 13; Mark1: 9
Jesus teaches in the synagogue	Luke 4: 16–30
Jesus thrown out of Nazareth	Luke 4: 28–29

As befits a pilgrimage route, the Nativity Trail was originally walked all the way from Nazareth. Purists may still wish to do that, though the route followed from Nazareth to Tabor and on to Faqu'a passes through suburbs and along roads, with very little to recommend it other than the ascent of Mount Tabor (R2). If you feel that using a vehicle to bypass the 'boring bits' is cheating, check out R4 and 5 before making your decision (and note that a vehicle is also recommended on Days 9 and 10 (R13 and 14)). Otherwise, like us, take the recommended way via R2 and 3. Either way, the first objective is:

MOUNT TABOR

'After six days Jesus took Peter, James, and John, with him and led them up the high mountain where they were all alone. There he was transfigured before them. His clothes became dazzling white, whiter than anyone in the world could bleach them. And there appeared before them Elijah and Moses, who were talking with Jesus.'

Mark 9: 2–4, Holy Bible, NIV

Tabor or Attour (meaning 'the high place') rises to 562m above the plain of Jezreel and Ibn Amer meadow (which is next to Diourieh village in the Galilee – the place where Jesus cured the epileptic boy). The mountain is about 9km SE of Nazareth and 19km SW of Tiberius (the Sea of Galilee). Its location on the junction of local roads with the ancient Via Maris between Egypt and Damascus has made Mount Tabor important since early times. Moreover, its unique shape captured the imagination of ancient peoples such as the Canaanites who attributed divine qualities to the mountain.

In biblical times the area around Mount Tabor was the scene of some fierce battles, such as the clash between Deborah and Barak's army on the mountain slope and the Sisera'a war chariots down in Jezreel Valley. It was also the scene of an incident in Gideon's battle against the Midianites, but the main claim of Mount Tabor to holiness stems from the Christian tradition that the Transfiguration of Jesus took place there.

Since the 4th century, Mount Tabor has been one of the holiest Christian sites in the Holy Land, with churches and monasteries being built, then a Crusader fortress, which fell to Sultan Baybars in 1263. In 1631 the Franciscans returned, and over the following centuries churches and monasteries were rebuilt. Also here is a chapel known as the Cave of Malchizedek, commemorating the curious Greek Orthodox tradition that the meeting between Abraham and Malchizedek, king of Shalem, took place here rather than in Jerusalem. Archaeological relics can be seen in the small museum, the key to which is kept by the church priest.

Arriving at the top, the visitor passes through the Gate of the Crusader fortress known as the Gate of the Winds. S of the gate are the remnants of the wall built by Josephus Flavius. The most prominent structure is the Franciscan Church, one of the most beautiful in the Holy Land. Two chapels flank its entrance – the one on the right is dedicated to Moses and the one on the left to Elijah to commemorate their presence during the Transfiguration. On the wall of the central apse of the church, above the higher altar, is a mosaic depicting the Transfiguration. The rock floor of the crypt is believed to be the spot on which Jesus stood during his transfiguration.

Accommodation Tabor Guest House (closed in winter)
tel: 06 673 5466

Some biblical references

Sacrificial offerings	Deuteronomy 33: 19
Abraham and Malchizedek	Genesis 14: 18–23
Deborah and Sisera	Judges 4: 4–16
Gideon's battle against the Midianites	Judges 8: 18
The Transfiguration of Jesus	Matthew 17: 1–2 and Mark 9: 2–9
Ahab in Jezreel	1 Kings 18: 41–46
Gideon at Harod and the Hill of Moreh	Judges 7
Elisha raises a woman's son	2 Kings 4: 8–37
Jesus at the foot of Mount Tabor	Mark 9: 14–29

The Nativity Trail commences with a tour of Nazareth including the Church of the Annunciation and the House of Mary then a drive out to the foot of Mount Tabor:

R2 Day 1, morning. The ascent of Mount Tabor

Short but sweet! A fairly steep ascent through thickly forested terrain to the summit of this holy mountain. Take your time, and enjoy the nature and the panoramic views that are unfolding around you as you climb.

Easy Walk: only 1.5km. Allow 1hr. 300m of ascent to the 562m summit, but fortunately plenty of forest shade along the way!

Special interest Tabor was occupied by Neanderthal man from 80,000 to 15,000BC when it was an important centre of the flint tool industry. Some caves, possibly in use during this period, are passed on the walk. In 1125BC, the Canaanite armies of King Hazor were defeated by the Israelites in the plain of Jezreel at the foot of Tabor. Other battles with Assyrians, Ancient Egyptians and Romans also took place in this militarily strategic location, close to Megiddo – which gave rise to the name 'Armageddon'.

Also nearby (to the SE) is the ruined Palestinian village of Indur – biblical Endor – where Saul was told by a 'witch' of the disastrous

Upper Wadi Qelt, site of a third-century monastery

View of Wadi Qelt and Bethlehem wilderness, with
the Jordan valley and Jericho beyond

Lower Wadi Qelt

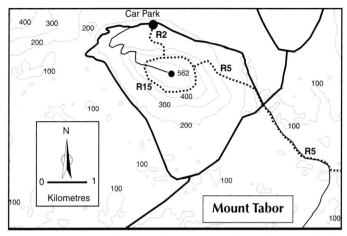

events that were to unfold at the imminent Battle of Gilboa, in which he and his army would be defeated by the Philistines.

From viewpoints on the walk, or from the ruins around to Basilica, it is possible to see Mount Hermon far to the N, beneath which is the location of the decisive Crusader–Muslim Battle of the Horns of Hittin. Lower still, and to the NE, is the Sea of Galilee in its hollow, but reputedly visible on a clear day. The Mediterranean is also supposed to be visible to the W (though it was too hazy to see either both times we were there).

Looking S, the hills of Gilboa rise beyond the plain of Jezreel. It seems everyone has fought a battle here, from Thutmose III at the Battle of Megiddo, via Alexander the Great and Napoleon to General Allenby in the First World War.

Some biblical references See above.

Flora and fauna The 'graceful', 'breast shaped' sacred mountain of Tabor stands in nubile isolation above the well-watered, fertile plain of Jezreel, which is rich in birdlife, especially during the seasonal migrations. Tabor itself is thickly forested, with evergreen oaks, terebinth, walnut, pine, carob, olive and other trees. In springtime the woodland glades are full of flowers and herbs such as wild thyme, purple thistles, mallows, hollyhock, golden broom, honeysuckle and convolvulus. There are also many birds and animals such as pigeons, eagles, partridges, foxes and even wolves.

Special advice Dress modestly and with respect for the holy places.

Mary Hartley

Gilboan Iris

Map SPNI 3

Map ref start 1863 2333; Map ref Mt Tabor 1867 2325

Approach Those not with a Nativity Trail group can go by bus from Nazareth, changing at Afulla for the infrequent connection to the car park at the bottom of the mountain. Better to take a special taxi.

The route Walk up by the wall on the R (W) side of the car park at the foot of the mountain. Continue in the same direction to find a path heading up the hill into the woods, with green trail-makers. It's heading for the tower, which is part of the church complex above and to the L, on the upper skyline.

Follow the path steeply S up the wooded hillside, eventually contouring L along a trail before rising again towards the summit. Just below the top, the trail meets the Mount Tabor Circuit (R15). The shortest way to the Basilica is to go R (W) and follow R15 for about 0.5km to the Gate of the Winds and thence up the road.

Return There are regular shuttle-taxis down the road, or walk, taking short cuts to eliminate some of the zigzags. Just over 1km back to the car park. Beware of the fast taxi drivers!

From here, the original walkers of the Nativity Trail (determined pilgrims that they were!) walked across the plain of Jezreel (see R5. Having been advised against 'a rather monotonous walk' we took the easy way by taxi, saving ourselves for the second climb of the day up the impressively steep northern slope of the Gilboa Hills:

R3 Day 1, afternoon. Jezreel to Faqu'a

A challenging scramble up the formidable N-facing barrier of the Gilboa Mountains takes you from the lush green sub-sea-level Jezreel Valley to the pine-clad rolling hills of the West Bank. Well worth the effort!

Moderate trek: not long, only 5 or 6km (plus another 3km if you have to walk from Road 71). Allow 3–4 hours from the tell in the Jezreel

Valley and another ½hr or so if you walk from Road 71. Over 400m of ascent to 430m, the first 250m being extremely steep with some scrambling (Grade 1). This makes a total of about 7–10km with 700m of ascent (about 5–6hrs) if you include it with R2 as the first day of the Nativity Trail – plus, of course, travelling time between the two routes. Not verified by the authors.

Special interest and biblical reference The hills S of the plain of Jezreel were the site of the biblical battle of Gilboa when the Philistines defeated Saul's army. 1 Samuel 31

Flora and fauna A short route but with considerable biodiversity, climbing steeply from below sea level in the green watery plain of Jezreel, rich in birdlife, to the dry limestone Eastern Hills of Palestine with their forests and olive groves.

Map SPNI 3

Map ref start 1883 2150; Map ref finish Faqu'a 1880 2108

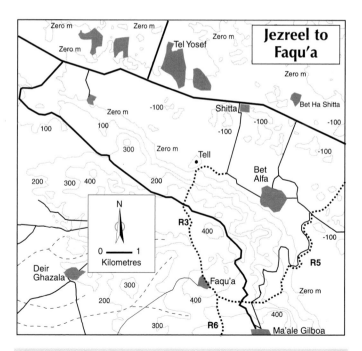

Approach Those not on the Nativity Trail should take a bus, servis or special from Nazareth to Afulla, then along Road 71 for 14km to the obvious Shitta Penitentiary! There is a road outside the R (W) wall of the prison. Follow this round S for about 2km between fields and pools. (If the road is closed to vehicles, you will have to walk.) Where it bends L (SE) a dirt track goes R (E). Follow it for 1km alongside an orchard until just before a tell. This is the drop off point for vehicles.

The route Follow the broad track S up the edge of the orchard then W along the hillside to a building where it ends. Continue across the steep rocky ravine and scramble up the hillside (some Grade 1), mostly on the R of the gorge, on the obvious path.

Where the angle eases, continue up through trees to reach a road just over 1km from the start but over

Mary Hartley

Mountain Tulip

300m higher! Cross the road and take the track S for just over 3km, turning R to enter Faqu'a. Or, better, leave the track after 1km and take any of the smaller paths up through olive groves towards the village and its minaret.

Return If you're on the Nativity Trail with a group you will be staying here in the village. It should also be possible to make your own accommodation arrangements beforehand (see below). Otherwise, you will need to take a special taxi to Nazareth or Nablus.

Those who decide to walk all the way from Nazareth to Faqu'a will probably arrive here two days later. This section of the route has only been walked by those who pioneered the trail and was not recommended. Below are some relevant notes, but for those who are determined to walk all the way to Bethlehem, the full description will be found on the website: www.birzeit.edu/nz2bl/trail.

R4 Day 1 alternative. Nazareth to Mount Tabor

From Nazareth, the route goes out E through the suburbs followed by a short but steep climb up the wooded slopes of Mount Tabor.

Moderate trek: 16km. Allow 6hrs. Not worthwhile except for the ascent of Tabor, which is very pleasant (see R2); however, determined pilgrims may wish to walk the whole route! There is about 350m of descent and 450m of ascent.

Special interest, biblical references, Flora and fauna See R2.

Map SPNI 3

Map ref Nazareth 1780 2337

Map ref Mt Tabor 1867 2325

Continuing with the alternative start to the Nativity Trail, the next two days cross the plain of Jezreel before climbing up to Faqu'a. Here are some brief notes (see website above for full information).

R5 Day 1 alternative. Mount Tabor to Taibeh and Faqu'a

Through Marj Bin Amer (Jezreel Valley), the fertile breadbasket of the region, to the village of Taibeh, then steeply up onto Mount Gilboa with splendid views of the valley below, before reaching the Palestinian village of Faqu'a.

Moderate trek. Approximately 43km. Allow two days. Although this is not a difficult walk and mostly follows well-defined tracks it is, according to the pioneers, 'gruelling and not so interesting'. The walk descends steeply from Mount Tabor at 562m to the Jezreel Valley, where it rises and falls to a low of 90m below sea level! It then climbs steeply again to 430m at Faqu'a: a total of about 700m of descent and 550m of ascent (give or take a few ups and downs). Instead of walking the entire distance in one day, it is best to do it over two, breaking your journey in Taibeh.

Special interest, biblical references, Flora and fauna See R2 and 3

Map SPNI 3 Also refer to maps with R2 and R3

Map ref start Mt Tabor 1867 2325

Map ref Taibeh 1920 2233

Map ref foot of Gilboa 1908 2105

Map ref finish Faqu'a 1880 2108

Whichever route you took (R2 and 3, or R4 and 5) you will now be in:

FAQU'A

The village of Faqu'a is just inside the 'Green Line' (see 'Politics and Religion' in the Introduction) and 430m above sea level. From it, you can see Nazareth, Mount Tabor, Marj Ibn Amir, the most fertile land in Palestine, and numerous other Palestinian villages. It is surrounded by beautiful dense woods where there is a ruin with caves and wells from which Faqu'a gets its name, dating back about 4000 years to Canaanite times. There are also cemeteries from the Roman and Byzantine eras, and many old water reservoirs carved into the rocks.

Mary Hartley

Crown Daisy

One can also see the remains of old olive and grape presses. The village was occupied in 1948 by Israel, losing over 35,000 dunums (about 9000 acres or 3600 hectares) of its land. Its mosque and school were destroyed and a large part of its land was occupied. As a result, many of its residents now have to work as labourers beyond the Green Line in Israel.

The area is in the transition zone on the edge of the 'Mediterranean zone', with around 500mm of rainfall and temperatures varying from 6°C (winter low) to around 20°C (summer high). In addition to the usual plants, the unique Faqu'a Iris and Faqu'a Aloe are found here. There are also aromatic fenugreek, assaries, chrysanthemum, mountain tulip and a wide variety of other wild flowers. The village land is filled with seed plants, legumes and fruit and olive trees. Faqu'a is also famous for its cactus fruits, which can be seen throughout the village.

Accommodation Head of Village Council (Ali Dhoukan) tel: 06 2433013;
Member of Village Council (Abdelqader Massad) tel: 06 2433037; and Hussni Massad tel:052 539368.

Shops general provisions

Medical facilities 1 clinic

Nearest town Jenin – 12km

Public transport   Morning and evening
Taxis   Frequent, from village centre to Jenin

If you are walking the Nativity Trail you should have had an enjoyable stay in Faqu'a and be ready for the next day of the trail (your second or possibly fourth, dependent on your choice of route from Nazareth). Or of course you can reach Faqu'a by taxi to enjoy the next day of the Nativity Trail as a one-day walk. It takes you through the Nablus Hills to the ancient town of Zababdeh, passing other old Palestinian villages along the way:

JALBUN

Known to the Romans as Gelbus, Jalbun, which is 325m abov1e sea level, is one of the most beautiful and serene villages in the area, with numerous wells and old houses in the midst of agricultural land with greenhouse crops and olive groves. Much of it is currently under Israeli control so that, as in Faqu'a, the residents have to work outside the Green Line. In the centre of the village is a cave with an arch at its entrance. Three other natural caves that were originally homes are now used as barns for livestock. The ancient shrine of Sheikh Ghasheem is in the centre of the village.

AL MUGHAYYIR

Further along the trail, at 300m above sea level, Mughayyir is well known for its agricultural products, such as olives and figs. The population, which includes Palestinian refugees from the 1948 war, also raises sheep and cattle for meat and dairy produce. Mughayyir boasts some of the most beautiful forests in the region, covering 400 dunums (about 100 acres or 40 hectares) of land, and these are used for charcoal. There are many archaeological ruins, including the remains of houses and water reservoirs carved into the rock.

Back on the trail again, we pass through these villages as follows:

R6 Day 2. Faqu'a to Zababdeh

'Breakfast arrived at 5.00am: locally produced hummus, lebaneh (thick, strained yoghurt) and tomatoes with freshly baked unleavened bread and mint tea, served on communal trays. With the sun rising behind a haze of clouds in Jordan we set off in the cool of the dawn, passing Palestinians waiting to be taken to work on nearby Israeli held land. Continuing down the grassy lane we passed through orchards and olive groves. Cactus and wild flowers grew in abundance: blood red

anemones, mountain tulips, swathes of yellow mustard and white crown daisies, blue and pink borage, pale purple flax, fenugreek and chrysanthemums. Carob trees offered patches of shade. Sage, thyme and camomile spread their delicate aromas – almonds were there for the picking.

We walked on through limestone dales where a shepherd with his herd of sheep, bells jingling in the silence, offered us tea, as is the custom. Overhead, buzzards searching for height to continue their springtime northern migration, spiralled on the thermals.'

'The Nativity Trail', Tony Howard, *Adventure Travel Magazine*, Sept 2000

A lovely segment of the journey, and a first experience of the Eastern Hills of Palestine. The trail leads through agricultural land and limestone dales, past the villages of Jalbun and Mughayyir, before reaching Zababdeh, a Christian town on the ancient Roman trade route.

Moderate trek: 20km, 8–9hrs, descending from 430m to just under 300m beyond Jalbun, then rising up to 430m again before descending to 200m and rising once more to the second pass at 400m and finally descending to Zababdeh at 330m. In all, 340m of descent and 240m of ascent.

Special interest   The hill country has always been populated by small villages. Through history, many armies have marched through this region (as referred to in the story of Joseph being sold into slavery, which took place in the neighbouring valley to Zababdeh). The hills were originally home to the Canaanites and Philistines, then in 931BC the area became the capital of the Northern Kingdom until it was besieged and conquered by the Assyrian Empire in 721BC. The occupants were consequently of mixed origin, and this formed the basis for the conflict between Samaritan Jews and those of Judah. Jesus is recorded as regularly teaching and preaching here.

Some biblical references

Joseph sold into slavery	Genesis 37: 12–24
Jesus heals ten lepers in a Samaritan village	Luke 17: 11–19

Flora and fauna   The rich agricultural land, olive groves and wild hills present a varied habitat for wildlife and birds. In springtime, wild flowers are abundant. (Also see notes on Faqu'a, above.)

Map   SPNI 3

Map ref start Faqu'a 1880 2108

Map ref Mughayyir 1865 2030

Map ref finish Zababdeh 1808 1992

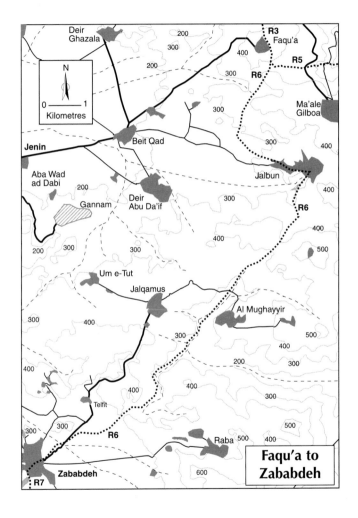

Mary Hartley

Hollyhock

Approach   Those not on the Nativity Trail could take a special taxi from Nablus or Nazareth, or a servis from Jenin.

The route   From the E side of the village, cross a small valley, past a cactus grove, then go R (SSW) along the old path on the side of the mountain, then slightly R across fields (ploughed, or with wheat dependent on the season). After 3km, and on the crest of the rise, turn SE towards Jalbun which will be seen in the valley ahead, and pick up the trail leading to the mosque with its tall minaret (5km). Go R at the mosque and take the track S closest to the hill then L at the Sheikh's

Tomb, keeping L into a valley. The track then rises up R to a saddle between rounded hills at 430m, 3km from Jalbun, then descends a pleasant valley for 2km SW to cross a country road beneath Mughayyir. About 4–5hrs.

Continue on the track down the valley to a fork in the wadi bed at 2km, where the main valley swings L (ESE) and another wadi enters from the R (W). Go up this pretty valley for 3km then, where it swings sharply L (E), go WSW over a pass and down the other side to meet a track going R (W) to meet Road 5827 almost 2km from the pass. Follow the road SW for 2km to reach Zababdeh.

If you are with a Nativity Trail group, the walk continues through Zababdeh for a further 1km W to the Naim Khader Community Centre where you will be staying overnight, allowing you to visit the old town.

Return   Those not staying overnight can go by taxi to Nablus or Nazareth (see below for information).

ZABABDEH

Situated about 330m above sea level, this is an important agricultural, grazing and dairy produce area. (The name may originate from the Arabic word for 'butter'.) It is an ancient village built on a Byzantine site. Zababdeh also has Roman ruins in the centre of town and was a significant Crusader site. The area still has strong Christian influence, with many schools and missions. A beautiful sixth-century church mosaic can be seen in the Church of the Rosary Sisters. The population is mixed Christian and Islamic and a model of indulgence and cordiality between faiths with shared participation in village life and religious occasions.

Zababdeh is in the 'Mediterranean' zone, with intermittent rainfall. The problem of water has increased as the residents are only allowed 20% of their water whilst the remainder goes to nearby Israeli settlements and military camps. Residents are not allowed to dig more wells, even in the area under PNA Control.

Employment is predominantly agriculture, with the usual crops of grains, pulses, vegetables and olives. There are also many greenhouses and, of course, fruit and almond trees, particularly beautiful in the spring. However, due to the Israeli occupation of the area there is a severe lack of employment; as a consequence many people work beyond the Green Line.

Biblical, historical and cultural tour   It is worth contacting Father Lewis Hazboun for a very enjoyable and fascinating tour of the town. Tel: 06 2510125 / 4.

Peter Hall

Old village well

General assistance
Mutie Daibis, Head of the Municipality of Zababdeh, can help if anything is needed, tel: 06 2510203 / 2. Father Lewis Hazboun (above) can also be of assistance.

Accommodation
Palestinian Agricultural Relief Committees (PARC), Centre of Martyr Nai'm Khader, tel: 06 2510462 / 1. To contact PARC directly, tel: Dr. Samir Al Ahmad 06 2436673.

Shops All provisions

Phones There are public phones in the shops that can be used by buying phone cards from the same shops.

Medical facilities
3 doctors: Dr. Milad Saleh, tel: 06 2510071; Dr. Walid Sharqawi, tel: 06 2510308; Dr. Malik Irshaid, tel: 06 2510447. Evangelical Clinic, tel: 06 2510033. Evangelical Clinic Pharmacy, tel: 06 2510174

Nearest town Jenin – 12km

Public transport Zababdeh bus company, tel: 06 2510306

Taxis Zababdeh is the centre for the surrounding villages, so a lot of taxis go to Jenin or Nablus.

From Zababdeh, the Nativity Trail heads SE over the hills through:

FARA'A (BIBLICAL TIRZAH)
Fara'a is about 10km NE of Nablus, close to biblical Tirzah, where flint tools have been found and pottery from the fourth century BC. Some of man's earliest attempts at dwellings were discovered here – semi-subterranean, with clay walls containing holes, possibly for inserting branches for roofing. Remnants of an early city from the Bronze Age (Canaanite Period) have also been found.

Tirzah was on Fara'a Hill with its grottoes, carved rocks and mosaic floors. Opposite are the ruins of Fara'a Tower with its ancient tunnel and pool. The Canaanite town was destroyed by Joshuah, son of Nun, in the 12th century BC, becoming the first capital of the Northern Kingdom. Six years later, King Omri transferred his capital to here. The wide valley of Tirzah is probably the way by which Abraham came to Nablus (Shechem) from Harran. The ancient occupation of Fara'a continued through the Iron Age until it was destroyed in 732BC by Assyrians, once more becoming a small village, which it remained into the Middle Ages.

Many of today's residents are refugees from historic Palestine, who lost their lands and houses to the Israeli occupation in 1948. There are three United Nations Relief Works Agency schools here. Despite its original ancient Palestinian heritage, this rich agricultural area also fell under Israeli occupation in 1967. The situation was then further exacerbated by subsequent settlements that not only benefit from and control the area's resources, but which caused many inhabitants to be exiled for a second time.

Some biblical references

Tirzah	1 Kings 14: 17–20, 15: 21–33 and 16: 16–24
Abraham's route to Shechem (Nablus)	Genesis 12: 5–6

R7 Day 3. Zababdeh to Agrabanieh

'Ahead lay the spring of Ain el Far'a in the Biblical land of Tirzah, the first capital of the Northern Kingdom. More significantly for us, was the opportunity for a mid-day swim in the pool of clear, cool water, followed by a cup of lemon tea whilst our friends relaxed in the shade, contentedly sucking on their nargilehs (hubbly-bubbly pipes).'

'The Nativity Trail', Tony Howard, *Adventure Travel Magazine*, Sept 2000

An enjoyable day over the Eastern Hills of Palestine then down to the broad sweep of Wadi Bidan, a picturesque and fertile valley rich in mountain springs.

Moderate trek: 21km, 8–9hrs (includes time for a swim). From 330m in Zababdeh, the trail ascends to 578m then (with a few ups and downs) descends to sea level at Agrabanieh (though it's difficult to believe). About 300m of ascent and 630m of descent.

Special interest and biblical references See Fara'a and Tirzah, above.

Flora and fauna Limestone hills and olive groves give way to the fertile Fara'a valley with its perennial springs watering lush orchards and rich agricultural land with diverse flowers, birds and wildlife.

Special advice If you intend swimming in the pool at Ain Fara'a, you will need swimwear (unless you are bathing in your clothes!). Women should not wear skimpy costumes. There is also a small café there.

Map SOIS map 6-111,1V

Map ref start Zababdeh 1808 1992; Map ref Ain Fara'a 1824 1884

Map ref finish Agrabanieh 1869 1823

Approach For those not on the Nativity Trail, the easiest way would be to take a taxi from Nablus, remembering to arrange to be met at Agrabanieh for the return journey!

The route From the centre of Zababdeh, go SE on the Nablus road, but before leaving town turn R (SSW) up a lane. Follow this up into the olive groves trending SSE then S though a saddle at 435m between twin tops. (The village of Sir can be seen on the hill to the R.) Continue S crossing a road, 3km from Zababdeh. Rise gently up through more olive groves to the shoulder of a hill at 578m, 2km to the SSE (excellent views), or descend S into a wooded valley at 400m and, still going S, climb up to the next top at 496m. (Just over 3km from the road, more good views.)

From either top, descend generally S to enter the narrow valley that can be seen ahead. Follow it, or its R shoulder, SSE down into orchards, beyond which is the road. You should arrive close to Ain Fara'a, below the hairpin bend. 12km, 5–6hrs, time for a swim!

From the spring, continue SE through citrus groves (the café proprietor will show you the path through the trees on the L of the stream). Quite soon, it rises up a little onto the L side of the valley, above the orchards, and crosses a side valley after 1km. Here, the terrain opens out onto the W shoulder of Jebel Tammun and a good track crosses a flat area of agricultural land SE for about 3km to meet the road in the bottom of Wadi Bidan. Either follow the road for just over 2km to a R fork which crosses the river, or descend to the river and follow paths along its bank (not as easy as it sounds!) to reach the same side-road. Follow it along the R bank of the river for 1.5km to the hamlet of Agrabanieh. Accommodation can be arranged in Aqrabanieh, or there is the option of orange grove camping.

Return Those not on the Nativity Trail should pre-arrange for a taxi (see below).

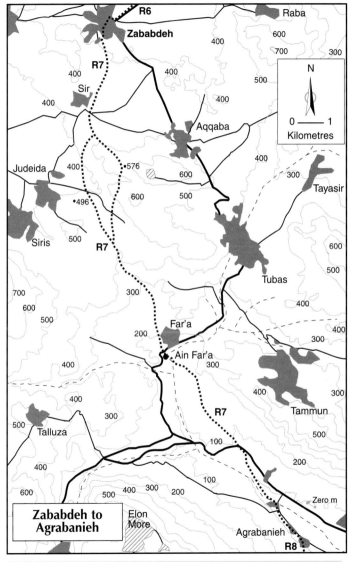

R6

Raba

Zababdeh

400

600

700

300

R7

400

N

500

Sir

400

400

400

Aqqaba

400

400

Judeida

400

•576

600

300

Tayasir

•496

600

500

400

Siris

500

600

500

R7

Tubas

700

600

500

300

Far'a

200

Ain Far'a

300

400

R7

300

400

300

Tammun

400

Talluza

300

500

100

200

500

600

400

300

200

100

Zababdeh to
Agrabanieh

Elon
More

Zero m

Agrabanieh

R8

79

AGRABANIEH ('THE PLACE OF SCORPIONS')

Situated above the edge of the Jordan Valley and exactly at sea level, the village is in Zone C, under Israeli control, but is expected to become Zone A (under Palestinian control) according to the Wye River Accord. It is a relatively new village, established in the early 1950s after its residents were expelled from the Palestinian Bir Shiva area in the 'naqba' of 1948. Most of the land of the village is not owned by the villagers, but belongs to two families from Nablus, with the residents sharing the produce with the landowners. There is one mosque and a mixed school run by the United Nations Relief Works Agency.

Accommodation   Mohammed Adel, tel: 052 346609
                   Basil abu Aqel, tel: 052 557739

Medical facilities 1 clinic

Nearest town Nablus – 15km

Taxis   Mohammed abu Aqel, tel: 050 234795
           Yousef Friah Ghanem, tel: 050 427645

Agrabanieh is dwarfed by high hills, the one to the S, Jebel Kabir ('Big mountain'), rising from sea level to 792m. After climbing this mountain, the trail then goes through two remote Palestinian villages:

BEIT DAJAN

Located in a high valley about 520m above sea level. The name may have Canaanite origins. The elders of the village say they are descendants of the Beni Sakhr, a large Bedouin tribe. The water supply is from wells and springs, usually far away as annual rainfall is quite low, often less than 450mm. The usual cereals and fruit crops are grown here; bees are raised for honey, and sheep and cattle for meat and milk. Nearby are various hamlets and a ruined castle. There is a shop in the village for mineral water and provisions, and you may even be invited for 'shai', as we were!

KHIRBET YANUN

This beautifully located hamlet nestles in a hillside hollow at 720m on the site of an ancient Arab Canaanite town, Yanouh. Today, most of its residents work as labourers within Israel. They are prohibited from constructing or repairing their buildings by the Israeli authorities, which has led to severe disrepair and a condensing of the existing homes. Making life even more difficult, two Israeli settlements were recently built on land appropriated from the village by the Israeli authorities, so the village has not only lost land, but the continuity of the water supply is also controlled by the settlers. The village is very poor, lacking electricity, roads, transportation and general public services, but, as you may well discover, the warmth of the people makes up for the lack of such facilities.

R8 Day 4. Agrabanieh to Yanun

The ascent of two mountains assures you of a physically challenging day rewarded with great views! You are also likely to experience the contrast of Palestinian hospitality in the villages along the way, with a close-up view of an anomalous hilltop Israeli settlement.

Moderate trek: about 15km, 6–7hrs, with 950m of ascent in two long steep climbs (the first of which is about 600m) and 300m of descent.

Special interest Big hills, panoramic views and contrasting cultures make this a challenging and fascinating day.

Flora and fauna The hills are covered in flowers in springtime. If you are lucky you will see the rare Nazareth Iris with its beautifully veined large purple flowers nestled high on the N slope of Jebel Kabir. Birdlife is plentiful. Raptors pass overhead on their annual migrations. The subterranean spring of Upper Yanun is teeming with fish.

Mary Hartley

Nazareth Iris

Special advice Start early for the 600m ascent to the pass of Jebel Kabir to avoid the heat of the day. Avoid the settlement above Yanun.

Map SOIS maps 6-111,1V and 9-1,11

Map ref start Agrabanieh 1869 1823; Map ref Beit Dajan 1852 1777

Map ref Yanun 1838 1726

Approach Those not on the Nativity Trail should take a taxi from Nablus, remembering to be met at Yanun for the return journey!

The route Head SW, directly up the hill for about 1km, before trending L to meet the skyline immediately below the long escarpment, which blocks a direct ascent of the hill (2km, possible Bedouin camp across to the R). Here, take care with route finding, and locate a path which goes up onto the nose of the lower cliff, then traverses R (NW) across it for 100m (exposed) before scrambling steeply up onto the upper slope. Continue up SW again to meet a good track which winds up first S, then SW, to reach the pass at 575m about 3.5km from the start. Follow the track enjoyably down to the welcoming village of Beit Dajan (6km).

As you approach Beit Dajan, you will see the minaret of a mosque in the centre of the town. Head towards this and also take your bearings from it when leaving the town. Take a good look at the hill on the horizon to the S of Beit Dajan, which you are going to climb – it's another big one! You will cross it at the low point that is immediately to the W of the large spur closest to Beit Dajan. This will help you to navigate your way through the olive orchards.

In Beit Dajan, go SW along the street below the village, soon leaving it for a rough track which rises SSW through olive groves before fading out. Continue across the shoulder of the hill at 560m and descend SW to a flat area of land in the olive groves. Continue SW on a dirt track to meet a good track heading W to the next hillside village of Beit Furiq. (The track was built in March 1999 by one of the Palestinian agricultural NGOs to give the Bedouin and farmers of Beit Dajan and Beit Furiq access to their lands in the Jordan valley to the E.) The final hill is now directly above you to the S (just over 3km from Beit Dajan).

Mary Hardley

Poppies

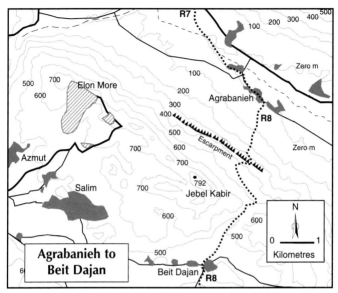

Agrabanieh to Beit Dajan

Walk W along the track until you are a few 100m W of the gully that leads up to the low point you saw from Beit Dajan. At the point of your choice, go L into the olive groves and steeply up terraces to meet a good track. This rises gently L across the hillside to enter the gully and join an old pack-animal track, which winds steeply up to the saddle at 815m. The track is now cut by a new and incongruous Israeli settlement of mobile homes, beyond which is the settlement road. A wire fence now cuts the old trail, so walk E along the side of the fence then turn S to meet the road. Cross it and follow the fence down, continuing slightly R down the rocky slope to meet the track again after it has re-emerged from the settlement. (It's an old Palestinian track that used to link the villages.)

Follow it down past olive groves to the old and pretty hillside village of Khirbet Yanun at 720m. Its spring (which is its only source of water) is on the SW side of the village, at the foot of the hill. If you are thirsty and there is no one around, walk up to one of the houses to introduce yourself and ask to use the water. This is more than a polite courtesy, as the settlers on top of the hill have been disrupting the water supply, causing considerable problems. Some people have spent the night

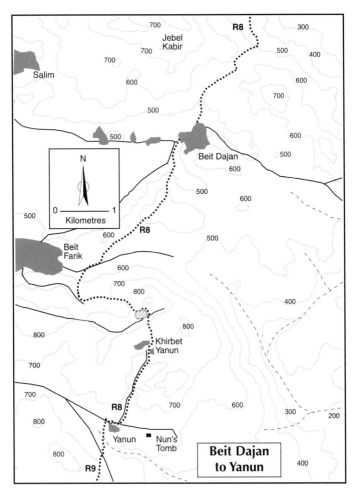

Beit Dajan to Yanun

here, as guests of the village, but it is usual to continue for another 1.5km down the village track to lower Yanun, another small and ancient hamlet.

Return If you are not walking the Nativity Trail or continuing to Duma, where there are more facilities (see R9), the only way out is by taxi to Nablus, which is best arranged beforehand. If, on the other hand, you are staying the night here, your early start will probably mean an early arrival; perhaps, like us, you will have some ornithological entertainment:

'As we relaxed in the warmth of late afternoon we were entertained by some birds on a nearby dead tree: on its broken top, a falcon was tearing at its prey, feeding its newly fledged young. A Syrian woodpecker tapped busily at the trunk. Lower down a goldfinch hid in the shade whilst on another branch a crow struggled to crack an almond held in its beak.'

'The Nativity Trail', Tony Howard, *Adventure Travel Magazine*, Sept 2000

YANUN

This small hamlet is owned by a Nablus family. The old house is similar to the traditional houses that include a stable area, but a second storey has been added. There is also a traditional 'taboun' bread oven. Fresh water is available from the spring. The name was derived from the prophet Nun, father of Joshua, whose tomb is visible less than 1km to the E, on a headland over 900m above the Jordan Valley (which at this latitude is 250m below sea level). There is ample space for camping, or, with prior arrangements, walkers can stay in an empty house in the hamlet and have food cooked by the locals.

Accommodation Ashraf Mohammad and Allam, tel: 052 908262

Nearest town Agraba 3km, Nablus 20km

Taxi Naim Nasser (in Agraba), tel: 052 491948

Biblical reference Book of Joshua and Deuteronomy 34: 9

From Yanun, another enjoyable but easier day on the hills follows:

R9 Day 5. Yanun to Duma

A shorter segment of the trail, along the high E edge of the fertile highlands, overlooking the arid slopes of the Jordan Valley, with the first glimpses of the Bethlehem Wilderness.

Easy walk: 12km. Allow 5hrs. About 140m of ascent and 170m of descent, finishing at 620m.

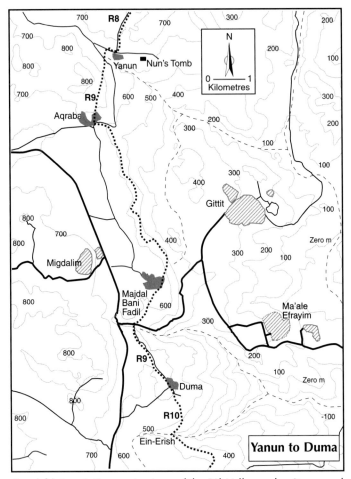

Yanun to Duma

Special interest Panoramic views of the Rift Valley and a site revered by the local people both add interest to this pleasant day on the hills.

Flora and fauna The hills are covered in flowers in springtime. Birdlife is plentiful. Raptors pass overhead on their bi-annual migrations up and down the Jordan Valley.

Map SOIS map 9-1,11

Map ref start Yanun 1838 1726; Map ref finish Duma 18491626

Approach Those not on the Nativity Trail should take a taxi from Nablus or Ramallah and arrange to be met at Duma for the return journey.

The route Looking SSW from Yanun, you will see a path going up from the valley below and just W of the hamlet to meet a narrow road which rises S over the brow of the hill – this is the way. From behind the hamlet, cross Wadi Juruf and head uphill, along the side of a gully, to the road. Cross the road and continue up the path onto the E shoulder of the hill. In the olive groves on the edge of the hill at about 750m is an old site called Sheikh Snoubar, with an old well, ruined buildings and trees with pieces of cloth tied to their branches: a local women's tradition as a thanksgiving for receiving a specific request. Without a local guide, the site is difficult to find, but the detour to the E, to the edge of the hill, is well worth the view to the Jordan Valley 1000m below.

The main path continues to head S down the hill into the village of Aqrabeh (almost 3km from Yanun). From the E side of Aqrabeh head SSE out of the village along the ridgeline of the low hill 0.5km E of and above the parallel road. Continue in this direction to the village of Majdal Bani Fadel at 670m, at the end of the ridge (6.5km from Agrabeh). Leave the village on the main dirt road, going S, soon reaching a T-junction.

Mary Hartley

Palestinian Arum

Turn R (SW) down to the highway, arriving at a T-junction. Cross over and continue up the small road for 2km into the village of Duma.

Return If you are not walking the Nativity Trail or continuing to Jericho (see R10) you will need a taxi to Ramallah, which is best arranged beforehand.

For those who are staying the night, after prior arrangement, hikers may camp either next to the village council centre or next to the girls' school. Meals can be arranged with local families.

DUMA

Canaanite, Roman, Christian and Muslim civilisations have all lived here. The name originates from an Arabic Canaanite word meaning 'silence and rest'. Known during Roman times as Adoma, the village overlooks the Jordan Valley, Jericho and the Dead Sea. Using binoculars it is possible to see Ar-Rabbad fortress (Ajlun Castle) on the mountains of Jordan. The village is famous for seeds, olives and grapes, and for its tradition of breeding cattle and sheep and making honey.

Like other villages on the eastern side of the Nablus Mountains, it is in the 'Mediterranean zone' with irregular rainfall (approx. 600mm yearly) and temperatures varying from 10°C (winter) to 2°C (summer). As always the water supply is from wells and springs, though it has been reduced as priority is given to the Israeli settlements in the area. There is a mosque in the village serving the predominantly Muslim population, built in the 7th century AD over the ruins of a Roman church. Other Roman ruins include pools and graves. There is also a ruined church with pillars, mosaics and carved gravestones. To the E of the village are the ruins of Deir al Muntar monastery.

Accommodation Habib Dawabshe (who can help with any arrangements between Yanun and Auja), tel: 052 625834

Shops Basic provisions

Medical facilities Dr Mahmoud Issa abu Raideh, tel: 052 290012

Nearest town Nablus – 27km

Taxi Yausif Salawda, tel: 052 528256

Nativity Trail walkers arriving early in Duma may like to take advantage of a hot, refreshing bath and massage in nearby Nablus (see R16) at this half-way point in their journey. It is easily arranged if you are with a group. We hope you will enjoy it as much as we did:

> *The object of our excursion was the Turkish bath built in 1480. We relaxed in the rest room, enjoying coffee, tea and kanafe – definitely yummy! In the baths, we sweated on the hot stone floor heated by underground fires in the Roman style. This was interspersed by dips in*

hot and cold water, then a steam bath that would put most saunas to shame. A cold shower followed, then back to the hot room for a final soap down and shower and out, tingling fresh (with a final massage if you want), ready for the next half of the walk.'

'The Nativity Trail', Tony Howard, *Adventure Travel Magazine*, Sept 2000

Suitably refreshed, another great day awaits you:

R10 Day 6. Duma to Ain Auja (Auja Spring)

'Scrambling down the dry waterfalls in this bare wilderness of rock we finally saw the tops of palms and figs trees ahead and heard a whispering and rustling of leaves. Or was it the sound of rushing water? A fast flowing stream appeared abruptly from beneath the rock. We plunged our hot feet into its refreshing coolness. There's nothing quite so magical as water in the desert – for we were now entering the 'wilderness' on the western fringe of the Jordan Valley.'

'The Nativity Trail', Tony Howard, *Adventure Travel Magazine*, Sept 2000

One of the wilder parts of Palestine, with contrasting scenery, first on rolling hills immediately above the Jordan Valley, then descending a deep and rugged gorge to reach the desert at the Spring of Auja.

Serious trek: 18km. Allow 7–8hrs. About 1000m of descent and 400m of ascent.
The route demands some route-finding ability to follow the best way along the hills and down the gorge. Ability to scramble on Grade 1 to 2 rock is also useful. Beware of flash flood risk in Wadi Auja and its approaches.
Maps SOIS 9-1, 11 and 9-111,1V
Map ref start Duma 1848 1626; Map ref high point 664m 1852 1568
Map ref finish Auja Spring 1867 1514. Also refer to map with R9.

Special interest The wild mountain scenery, sweeping panoramas, great views of the Jordan Valley and the scramble through the rocky gorge are the real attractions of this day on the hills. Those interested in biblical history may also be interested to know that the first-century BC Fortress of Sartaba (Alexandrion) is on the easily seen conical hill down below in the Jordan Valley. It gained its macabre name ('Fortress of the slayer') due to the high number of people killed by its builder, the Maccabaean prince Alexander Jannaeus. Later, Herod renovated the site and ensured it retained its grim reputation. In his inimitable style he had two of his sons strangled and buried here, along with his wife Mariamme's brother, whom he had drowned. Nice guy!

Flora and fauna In springtime, the hills are green and full of flowers. Birdlife is abundant, especially if you are there when vast flocks migrate up the Jordan Valley. In the autumn when the hills are burnt brown the land is harsher and less forgiving. Even then, we saw rock hyrax and a tortoise and always the flute-playing Bedouin shepherds wandering the hills with their donkeys and flocks of sheep and goats, giving the land a unique timeless appeal.

Special advice The hills are almost bare of shade, so carry plenty of water especially on hot days. In the winter season remember that the gorge of Wadi Auja can flood after rain.

Approach To reach Duma from Jerusalem, you can take a servis taxi to Nablus via Ramallah, then on to Duma; but, though this is the cheapest way, it's time consuming. A better alternative is to take the servis to Ramallah (6NIS each) then a special to Duma (for which we paid 70NIS). The taxi departure point in Ramallah is Mujam'aa on Shara el Irsal, 100m E of Manara Square (the one with the fountain and lions). The taxi stand is alongside El Bireh Shopping Centre and the Lebanese Restaurant. If you are prepared to spend a little more, it's around 100NIS for a special from Jerusalem. Whichever way you go, it may be useful to have a road map with you to show the driver where Duma is! Once there, the road passes though the village centre, bending to the L at the far end, with a girls' school R of the bend.

The route Walk S out of the village down the track R of the school, leaving it for a path which goes R, through fields and down between boulders to Ain Duma spring in the narrow valley of Wadi al Rashrash (just over 1km).

Continue down steeply from the spring, on a small path, cross the stream bed and scramble back up the far side to gain a path on a limestone terrace. Follow this pleasantly SE, past a spring watering trees on a terrace below, and contouring along the hillside to a shoulder (alt. 500m).

Continue round, rising as you go, across the undulating hillside to drop into a valley and ascend a wide track up its bed to a T-junction near the top. Go L (SE) and follow the track round and uphill SW, leaving it to cross the hillside on its L (alt. 570m) in a more S direction. (Settlement visible to the W.) Also visible directly ahead (S) is another broad track – head for it, descending steeply into a valley to meet it near the bottom. About 2hrs from the start, 6km, alt. 450m.

It's a steady uphill walk on the track (or taking short cuts) to reach a saddle at 600m, after about 1km, T-junction. Take the R track and continue up to a col and high plateau probably with Bedouin camps and fields beyond (alt. 630m). Here, an obvious track goes sharp L and slightly downhill. Another less well-defined track rises gently uphill SSW towards a high point (664m). Follow it, for a very enjoyable 2km across the breezy upland ridge with excellent panoramic views, especially into the Jordan Valley immediately below. The conical hill of Sartaba is clearly visible, whilst further E across the Jordan River, the hills of Gilead can be seen and the gash of the biblical valley of the Jabbok below Roman Jerash.

Towards the end of the plateau, pass just R of the penultimate top then well L of the final one (690m), keeping in the same SSW direction and descending to a track which starts by some Bedouin caves with some welcome shade. Follow this track S over a small hill. Beyond, cross a road and descend S towards a valley on the L. Either enter it immediately via a steep descent on loose terrain to a track in its bed or walk along its R shoulder, descending into the valley where another wadi meets it from the R after 0.5km or so. Tree and shade. 4½hrs, about 12km.

Follow the valley down enjoyably on the limestone riverbed, with some scrambling (Grade 1 and 2), or bypass the tricky bits with care a little higher up on the side of the valley. After another ½hr the riverbed plunges over cliffs marked by a photogenic pinnacle into the depths of Wadi Auja.

It's now about 5km to Auja Spring. To reach it, go R on ledges between a rock tower and the cliff, then descend steeply to the riverbed below. Follow it down through boulders for ½hr or so (some scrambling, Grade 1 and 2) to an area where recent rock falls from the hillside on the R have filled the valley with small boulders. A little further on, a big wadi enters from the R, after

Mary Hartley

Palestinian Pheasant's Eye

which the path crosses the riverbed to the L side, continuing for another ½hr or so to the spring (fast flowing in springtime, but maybe non-exis-

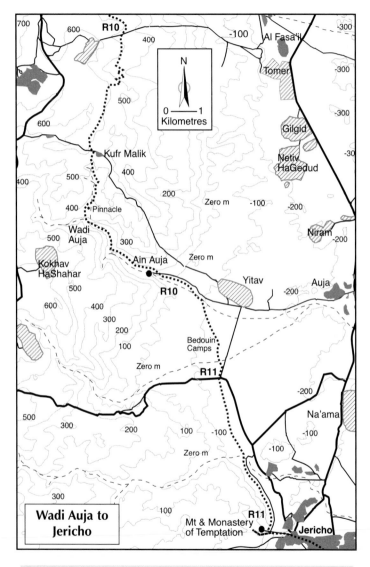

Wadi Auja to Jericho

tent by the autumn!). You are now at sea level. Continue alongside the tree-filled riverbed to meet the road in 5mins.

The return If you are not on the Nativity Trail, you should pre-arrange to be met by a taxi (see notes below), otherwise it's another 6km down the road to reach the Jericho–Ramallah road, where you should be able to get a servis. (Turn R after 2km, then L (SSE) along a trail through the desert to meet the highway.)

On the other hand you may be as lucky as us – when we reached the road near the spring there was no one around except a Bedouin enjoying a beer, with his empty taxi parked nearby. We got a free cold beer and lift to Ramallah for 80NIS – that was at the time of the October 2000 'Al Aqsa Intifada' when Israeli roadblocks were everywhere and travel was tricky. You might improve on the price – though you may not get a free beer! Thinking of which, if you return to Ramallah, you will pass close to the Taybeh Beer factory; if it's weekend and not too late, why not call in for a free factory tour and 'sample'! Friday and Saturday 11.00–18.00. Tel: (02) 2898868
Website: www.taybehbeer.com

If you're on the Nativity Trail you can walk to your overnight stop in the desert (it's not far away), or your Palestinian Travel Agent will meet you met at the road-head and drive you to the Bedouin Camp. Otherwise you need to camp or pre-arrange accommodation (see below).

AUJA

Famous for its springs, which were familiar to Stone Age man who lived in nearby caves, Auja was also on the route of a Roman road. These days, it is accessible by a number of routes, including a mountainous road which descends a beautiful valley from Kufr Malek and Samia's Spring in the hills near Ramallah, as well as from nearby Jericho. Traditionally Palestinian, it fell under Israeli control in 1948.

Because of the abundance of water, warm climate (17–30°C) and the fertility of the land, the villagers are able to harvest citrus fruits and bananas. Al Auja Spring is one of the most important springs in the region due to its continuous water supply, critical in area of very low rainfall. It begins in a sugarcane plantation then passes through natural rock formations with numerous wild plants, including mallow and 'canal peppermint'. The water is used for crop irrigation and is distributed according to traditional arrangements. Laurel trees also grow widely within the valley, in addition to lotus jujube trees, the wood of which farmers use to make their ploughs and other agricultural tools, as well as for fuel.

Many of the inhabitants are from well-known Bedouin tribes, which are also found in Jordan and Sinai. Additionally, in Lower Auja (Taht Auja) there are also about 8000 refugees who form the bulk of the labour force. The whole of the Jordan Valley is classified as an Israeli 'settlement zone' with no significant Arab presence – 15 settlements have already been established around Jericho. Auja has been considerably affected by the occupation, which not only defines the infrastructure but also makes it a struggle for the Palestinians to retain their traditional livelihood, religion and culture.

Biblical reference Nearby ruins and remains of aqueducts from biblical Senaa. Ezra 2: 35

Nearest town Auja village – 5km, Jericho – 10km

Accommodation To overnight with Bedouin, contact: Suliman abu Dahouk, tel: 052 649404

Public transport See notes on Jericho following R11. There is no reception for mobile phones at Ain Auja, so if you need assistance, you need to walk down the road some way before you can call.

Peter Hall

Bedouin Camel,
Jordan Valley

SARTABA

If you want to hike to Sartaba (mentioned above) the way is from the Jordan Valley. It's necessary to phone the Isreali Defence Force (IDF) for permission as, even though it's in Palestine's West Bank, it is in an Israeli firing range, tel: 02 5305252 or 02 5305372. (We tried, but no one answered the phones although they are supposed to manned 24hrs a day.)

Having spent the night in the desert at a Bedouin camp, those on the Nativity Trail now head for Jericho, via:

THE MOUNT OF TEMPTATION

'Directly west, at the distance of a mile and a half, is the high and precipitous mountain called Quarantania, from a tradition that our Saviour here fasted forty days and forty nights, and also that this is the "high mountain" from whose top the tempter exhibited 'all the kingdoms of the world, and the glory of them'. The side facing the plain is as perpendicular, and apparently as high as the rock of Gibraltar, and upon the very summit are still visible the ruins of an ancient convent. Midway below are caverns hewn in the perpendicular where hermits formerly retired to fast and pray in imitation of the "forty days" and it is said that even at the present time there is to be found an occasional Copt or Abyssinian languishing out his quarantania in this doleful place. We found it, however, inhabited only by Bedawin, several of whom made their appearance, well armed, many hundred feet above us.'

The Land and the Book, W. M. Thomson, 1876

The Mount of Temptation is no longer home to armed 'Bedawin' (though they would be more exciting than the tourists who arrive by the incongruous cable car!). Originating in the 12th century, the monastery devoted to Christ's 'forty days in the wilderness' is well worth visiting. On the top of the mountain, at 100m, are Selucid and Hasmonean ruins, mingled with those of an unfinished 19th-century church. The views over Jericho to the Dead Sea are superb.

Biblical reference
Jesus tempted in the wilderness Luke 4: 1–15 and Mathew 4: 1–11

R11 Day 7. Auja to Jericho

Desert terrain leads to the Mount of Temptation with its Orthodox monastery clinging to the rocky cliffs adjacent to the new and (in our opinion) unsightly cable car station. Having climbed to the summit, the trail descends to Jericho, 'the oldest city on Earth'.

Easy walk: 13km. Allow 5hrs to include the monastery visit and the summit of Jebel Quruntal at 100m (350m above Jericho, 400m above the Jordan River). Starting from sea level, about 120m of ascent and 370m of descent.

Special interest, biblical references See above. Also, to the E of the track to the foot of Quruntal, there is the site of the ancient Jewish village of Na'aran mentioned in Joshua and Chronicles as one of the villages bordering the territory of Ephraim. The remains of a sixth-century synagogue include a fascinating mosaic floor. Though ultra-Orthodox Jews have defaced many of the pictures, there remains a superb image of a deer or gazelle, with images reflecting a passage from the Song of Songs 2: 8–13.

Flora and fauna You may well see raptors and other birds soaring on the thermals and rock hyrax on the cliffs. The orchards of Jericho are spread out below, in the Jordan Valley:

> 'Citrus is the main produce, though it was only developed after 1948 when the Palestinians could no longer reach their groves in Jaffa. Some of the larger orchards have their own Artesian wells, but usually water comes from the spring and is "bought" with the house. When it gushes along the channels by the roadside, the house-owner or gardener is allowed to open the sluices to his garden for twenty minutes per week and soak the ground around the trees.
>
> The Jericho orange is one of the most delicious of any country: ovular rather than spherical, it has a very thin inner skin and taste that is neither too sharp nor too sweet. Some people call it a "Cleopatra" after the enchanting Queen who was given land in the valley by her Roman lover Mark Antony. But there were no oranges there in her day. Sweet-smelling balsam was the main produce. Now bananas are second in importance to the citrus: the Jericho banana is small but sweet and mellow. Devastated by frost some years ago, the groves have been replanted and are doing well. Sometimes one sees a gazelle peering shyly from between the huge frayed leaves.'

Jericho – Oasis Town, Delia Khano, 1998

Special advice Dress with respect for the holy places and Palestinian tradition.

Map SOIS 9-111,1V

Map ref start near Auja 1883 1500

Map ref, Mt of Temptation 1908 1425

Map ref finish Jericho 1935 1404

Also refer to map with R10

Approach This route would not normally be walked other than by those on the Nativity Trail, except for the ascent of Jebel Quruntal, which is directly accessible from Jericho.

The route From the Bedouin camp in the desert S of Auja Spring, head S up the rise for an excellent view or, more easily, avoid the hill by

Walking through Wadi Zerqa

In the hills near Zababdeh, Nativity Trail

On Jebel Kabir above Agrabanieh, Day 3 of the Nativity Trail

Walking up from Yanun, which is visible below, Day 5 of the Nativity Trail

Leaving Beit Dajan, Day 4 of the Nativity Trail

High above the Jordan Valley, Day 6 of the Nativity Trail

taking the path on the R. Continue S, crossing a road (just over 2km) with the remnants of an ancient aqueduct on the R. Continue S, up and down small hills, possibly passing several Bedouin camps. Stay on the track past the camps and a water tank to reach a wire fence (1½–2hrs). Go R of this, and continue SSE along the good track at the foot of the mountains for another ½hr, passing a water station and reaching the village of Ain Duke. (The sixth-century synagogue is across the wadi to the E.) The track then continues to the foot of the Mount of Temptation (9km).

Join the pilgrims and tourists on the path to the upper cable car restaurant, from where the way goes L into the Monastery of Temptation, which hangs like swallows' nests from the cliffs. Continue past monastic caves where it is said that Jesus may have fasted and resisted the devil, then up a steep narrow path to the summit. Spiritually and physically replete, descend and follow the road SE for 3km into the centre of Jericho, where there is a choice of restaurants and accommodation. Walkers of the Nativity Trail may also camp in orange groves or stay overnight in a nearby monastery:

ST GERASIMUS GREEK MONASTERY
The site of biblical Beth Hoglah (Deir Hajla in Arabic) is a tranquil location with a trellis of vines covering its central courtyard. St Gerasimus was the first to combine the life of the wilderness hermit with the founding of a monastery in the Jordan Valley in 451AD. He reputedly lived in a cave with a lion as companion, as did a later hermit in the 12th century, when the present monastery was founded.

It is located about 7km SE of Jericho towards the Jordan River (not far from the Jordan River Baptismal Site) and about 7km from the Dead Sea. Rooms vary from 50 to 100NIS. Evening meal is about 15NIS. There is also a pleasant outside café and bar, and self-catering facilities. Access by taxi from Jericho. Book in advance (see below).

Some biblical references
Beth Hoglah	Joshua 15: 6, 18: 19–21
Baptism of Jesus	John 1: 4–12

JERICHO
Archaeological investigations reveal that Jericho, sometimes designated the oldest town in the world, was first settled about 8000BC. The first biblical mention of Jericho is the account of the entry into the land of Canaan by the Israelites, led by Joshua, after the Exodus from Egypt

Peter Hall

Ancient millstones

about 1250BC. Jericho also appears regularly in the stories of the prophets Elijah and Elisha. In the first century BC, with its mild climate and fertile land, it became the favoured location for winter palaces for the Hasmonean and Herodian kings, the ruins of which remain today. Jesus passed through Jericho several times on his journeys from Galilee to Jerusalem, and a number of well-known gospel events took place here. Jericho remained an important Arab town in the Byzantine, Arab and British periods, and is today an important centre for the Palestinian people. If you fancy joining the locals for a coffee and *nargileh* whilst the sun sets, it is just as famous now for its hospitality, street cafés and relaxed atmosphere as it was over a hundred years ago:

'Then comes the solemnity of coffee and smoking, with a great variety of apparatus. Some use the extemporaneous cigarette, obviously a modern innovation. Others have pipes with long stems of cherry or other wood, ornamented with amber mouthpieces. The argeleh with its flexible tube of various-coloured leather, seems to be the greatest favourite. Some of these are very elegant. The tube of the one brought me the other evening was at least sixteen feet long, of bright green leather, corded with silver wire; the bottle, or kuzzazeh, as you call it, was very large, of thick cut glass, inlaid with gold, really rich and beautiful. I however, could produce no effect upon the water in the bottle. One needs a chest deep as a whale, and powers of suction like another maelstrom, to entice the smoke down the tube, through the water, and along the coiled sinuosities of the snake, or nabridj; and yet I saw a lady make the kuzzazeh bubble like a boiling caldron without any apparent effort. The black coffee, in tiny cup, set in holders of china, brass, or silver filigree, I like well enough, but not the dreadful fumigation. A cloud soon fills the room so dense that we can scarcely see each other, and I am driven to the open court to escape suffocation.'

The Land and the Book, W. M. Thomson, 1876

Some biblical references

Exodus from Egypt	Joshua 4: 19
The healing of two blind beggars	Matthew 20: 29–34
The healing of blind Bartimaeus	Mark 10: 46–52
Zacchaeus the tax collector	Luke 19: 1–10

Accommodation

St Gerasimus Monastery	Tel: 02 9943038 or 050 348892
Intercontinental Hotel	Tel: 02 231 1200; Fax: 02 231 1222 E-mail: jericho@interconti.com
Al Quds Jerusalem Hotel	Tel: 02 232 2444; Fax: 02 992 3109
Jericho Resort Village, Hisham's Palace	Tel: 02 232 1255; Fax: 02 232 2189 E-mail: marketing@jericho-resort.com

Shops, restaurants and cafés In abundance!

Medical facilities Hospital, tel: 02 2321966 / 9

Public transport Bus and servis

Taxis Abu Majed Taxi, tel: 052 679457; Qasar Hisham Taxi, tel: Jericho 02 2322129; Petra Taxi, tel: Jericho 02 2322525

THE DEAD SEA

Jericho is close to the Dead Sea (just ½hr by taxi). Walkers on the trail may take the opportunity to experience the bizarre pleasures of floating in the world's lowest lake at 400m below sea level whilst they contemplate the barren hills and biblical history of the Bethlehem Wilderness which they will be crossing the following day, starting up the impressive:

WADI QELT

This spectacular gorge descends from E of Jerusalem down to Jericho. The ancient Roman road from Jerusalem to Jericho follows its S rim and is a route with which Jesus and his disciples would have been familiar. It is believed that this gorge, which is notoriously dangerous, inspired the words of Psalm 23:

'Even though I walk through the valley of the shadow of death, I will fear no evil'.

In the third and fourth centuries AD this area became a centre for desert monasticism, and the caves of hermits still dot the cliffs (see below, and R23 to R27).

MONASTERY OF ST GEORGE OF KOZIBA

The spectacular Monastery of St George of Koziba is in Wadi Qelt, on the route of the Nativity Trail. Founded in 480AD, the monastery houses the cave associated with Elijah. It was sacked by the Persians, renovated by the Crusaders, then once more abandoned. A Greek monk, Kalanikos, restored it once more in the late 1800s. A visit to it is essential. (And the free cold fruit drinks are very welcome – don't forget to leave a contribution to the monastery!)

Some biblical references

The valley of the shadow of death   Psalm 23

Parable of the Good Samaritan   Luke 10: 25–37

Elijah's encounter with God   1 Kings 19: 9–14

From Jericho, refreshed and relaxed (that's if you didn't spend the night – and all your money – in the casino!), we head once more for the hills:

R12 Day 8. Jericho to Nebi Musa

Rocky canyon, barren desert, historic Jewish, Christian and Islamic sites combine to make a unique and varied day. The walk up to St George's and the Roman road above is probably the most popular 'wilderness' walk in this guide, wild and rugged, but on a good trail. Beyond are the bare desert hills, through which the trek then passes to reach the Muslim shrine of Nebi Musa.

Moderate trek: 14km, about 5–6hrs, dependent on the time spent in St George's. The walk rises from minus 250m at Jericho to minus 100m at St George's then up to a high point of 80m (480m above the Dead Sea) before descending desert hills (with some minor ups and downs) to Nebi Musa at 100m below sea level. In all, about 350m of ascent and 200m of descent.

Special interest Herod's Winter Palace, hermit caves, the magnificently situated fifth-century Monastery of St George of Koziba (see above), one of the most spectacular sights in Palestine, and the desert shrine of Nebi Musa (see below) make this a fascinating day.

Flora and fauna In Wadi Qelt you are likely to see rock hyrax and, of course, lizards and other small creatures. Also, there are Cypress trees and other vegetation around the monastery that, together with the perennial stream, provide a good habitat for birdlife. Once onto the desert hills, it's another world, bare and windswept – enjoy the contrast!

Peter Hall

Monastery of St George, Wadi Qelt

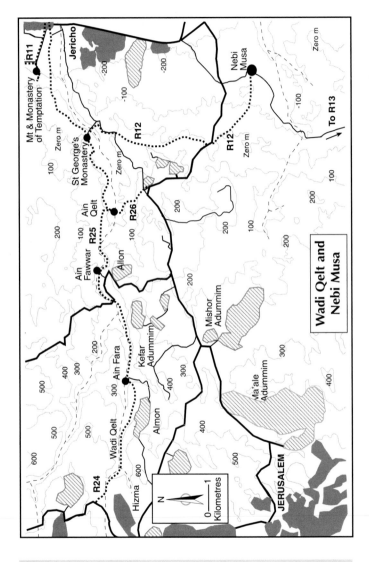

Wadi Qelt and
Nebi Musa

Special advice Dress with respect for the holy places, as well as for the terrain. The latter half of the journey is hot and dry – carry adequate water.

Map SPNI 8

Map ref start Jericho 1935 1404; Map ref St George's 1890 1390

Map ref finish Nebi Musa1910 1328

Approach Start from Jericho, or be lazy and take a servis out to the foot of Wadi Qelt to save 2km!

The route From Jericho walk out W along the road for 2km across the plain towards Wadi Qelt – the visible gash in the mountains ahead. The ruins of Herod's Palace are on the right (N) just before the entrance to the wadi. The path then winds up into the savage gash of the canyon where aqueducts and hermitages can be seen as the trail winds up through the cliffs. Eventually, the dramatically located monastery is seen in the distance. After enjoying a cold refreshing drink or a coffee or tea, you can visit the beautiful chapel with its holy relics (including the body of St George of Koziba, the founder of the monastery, and an ossiary of other martyrs) (5km; allow 2hrs, more to include the monastery visit).

From the monastery, the path descends to cross the gorge by a bridge, then rises up through the cliffs (excellent views of the monastery) to reach a car park with souvenir and snack stalls on the old Roman road (5mins).

Walk up the road for almost 1km to a viewpoint on the R down into Wadi Qelt. Beyond here, the trek rapidly becomes more serious.

Go diagonally L (SSW) on desert paths and tracks, rising away from the road to reach a wide track along a ridge with a steep drop to the L. Follow the track towards a mast on the summit of a hill at 162m. About 0.25km before reaching it, take shepherds' tracks across the very steep slope directly below it to its E (exposed). Having crossed the slope with care, follow more shepherds' paths SSE down into desert valleys and over small hills to reach a small road after about 2km. Follow this R (S) for about 1km, then descend directly to the main Jerusalem–Jericho road.

To the S are small desert hills. Leave the road and cross them heading SE, rising and falling, in and out of shallow valleys for 1km to a little top at minus 39m(!). Nebi Musa is 1km E of here; the first view of it will give you a true appreciation of its location, nestled in the folds of the Bethlehem Wilderness (though it is now, of course, accessible by road).

Return For those not on the Nativity Trail, it's only 1.5km N along the road to the Jericho–Jerusalem highway, so you could walk there to get public transport or phone for a taxi to Jericho (see information above). Those on the trail will be staying the night in the shrine, where food is also provided.

NEBI MUSA

'O Moses! I have chosen you in preference to others, and entrusted you with the mission to convey My words as contained in My revelations to all the people around, and to join the ranks of these who are grateful to Me.'

The Holy Qur'an, surah 7, verse 144

The Muslim shrine and pilgrimage site of the Maqam Al Nebi Musa (the Tomb of the Prophet Moses) is directly opposite Mount Nebo in Jordan. According to Old Testament tradition and just prior to his death, Moses looked across at 'the promised land' from Mount Nebo, which is above the N end of the Dead Sea. Dating from 1269, there is an Arabic inscription over the tomb: 'The construction of this maqam over the grave of the Prophet who spoke with God, Moses, is ordered by His Majesty Sultan Thaher Abu Al-Fateh Baybars in the year 688 Hijra.'

The nearby mausoleum is said to be that of A'isha, Mohammed's favourite wife, whilst almost 1km SW along the road is the *maqam* of Hassan al-Rai, the shepherd of Moses. Though there is considerable doubt about the authenticity of these sites, there is no doubt that this is a perfect location for the contemplation of the death of Moses. The epitaph of the 13th-century Sufi mystic Jalaludin Rumi fits the bill perfectly:

'When we are dead, seek not our tomb in the earth, but find it in the hearts of men.'

For 800 years, the shrine has been the focus of a massive annual Muslim pilgrimage from Jerusalem's Al Aqsa Mosque, coinciding with the Holy Week of the Eastern church preceding their Easter and concluding with five days of prayers and festivities.

Some biblical references

Moses and the journey from Egypt	Exodus, chaps. 2–3
Moses returns to Egypt, and the plagues	Exodus, chaps. 4–12
Crossing the Red Sea	Exodus, chap. 14
The Ten Commandments	Exodus, chaps. 19–20
Death of Moses	Deuteronomy 32:48–34:12

Accommodation   Sheikh Mohammed Jamal
                      Tel: 052 246180 / 052 910422

Shops Café and souvenirs

Nearest town Jericho 10km

Taxis See notes on Jericho above

Having spent the night at Nebi Musa, the Nativity Trail sets off once more into the wilderness of the dry Bethlehem Hills. This region in particular, but to some degree all such desert areas, play an important part in the social and religious life of the people of the Near East. Traditionally, the desert wilderness is seen as a place of encounter with God, where the forces of evil can be confronted and, with His assistance, overcome. The prophets of old lived in and emerged from the desert, and saints of every age have often gone to spend time there. The desert is a symbol of a spiritual wilderness: there is a paradox between the profound stillness and emptiness of the desert and the sense of life and energy that it evokes. The Bible is full of imagery of waters flowing in the wilderness and the desert coming to life. It was into the desert that Jesus went to be alone with God, to reflect on his mission, to be prepared for his ministry and to be tempted by the devil.

Some biblical references

Psalm 107: 33–38, Isaiah 35: 1–2, Isaiah 40: 3, Luke 4: 1–13

Those who zealously walked the trail all the way from Nazareth, avoiding the option of a vehicle to reach Mount Tabor and cross the Jezreel plain will now be ready for their 11th day. Here again, they have a decision to make: they can join the 'softies' (either those who have been tempted by the devil, or the sensible – whichever way you care to look at it!) and take a vehicle 12km S along the rather boring desert road to the accepted start of the next day's trek or they can walk it. (You know which we did!) The objective is another magnificent holy place in an even wilder situation:

THE MONASTERY OF MAR SABA

The monastery was founded by St Saba in 482AD, prior to which he lived in a cave in the gorge (now identified by a cross and the letters AC). Despite its sacking by Persians in the seventh century, the monastery was destined to become one of the largest in the Holy Land. Unbelievably, its population once approached 5000! In 1834 it was severely damaged in an earthquake, but later renovated to its present splendour. Nowadays, only a few monks remain, living an ascetic life. The bones of the 400 martyrs of the Persian onslaught are kept in the

Peter Hall

The monastery of Mar Saba on the cliffs of the Qidron Gorge

cave church. The body of Mar Saba lies behind glass at the entrance to the newer church. There is also a 'dining-room' where a drink and sweets are available. Across the Qidron Gorge numerous hermitage caves can be seen – including that used by St Saba.

Opening times are usually 8.00 to 16.00 Sunday to Thursday (men only). These times cannot be guaranteed. It is best to check beforehand by phoning.

R13 Day 9. Nebi Musa to Mar Saba

'My eye roamed over a wilderness of rusty brown hills, the most dreary and blasted that I ever beheld. Beyond and below it is the Dead Sea bordered on the east by the abrupt cliffs of Moab. Turning to what was beneath me, the wonderful chasm of the Kidron struck me with amazement. We have seen nothing so profound or so wild in all our travels...

Saint Saba was probably attracted to the spot by those very savage aspects of the scene which strike our minds with such horror. The howling wilderness, the stern desolation, the terrific chasms, the oppressive solitude, the countless caverns, the ever-prevalent dangers from wild beasts and wild robbers – these and such as these were the charms that fascinated his morbid imagination'

The Land and the Book, W. M. Thomson, 1876

This is a real desert trek though harsh, unforgiving hills with their own rugged beauty, and connecting some unique religious and historical sites.

Moderate trek: 8km. Allow 4hrs. About 350m of ascent overall and 100m of descent, finishing at 250m. After driving S from Nebi Musa, the walk starts from 60m above sea level in the Bethlehem Wilderness. On a hot day, it is more arduous than its short distance would suggest.

Special interest The first objective is the isolated Hasmonean (second century BC) fortress of Hyrcania, also known as Khirbet Mird, standing aloof and alone on a wild commanding hilltop in the heart of the desert hills. Here are the remains of aqueducts, wells and pools with a storage capacity of 20,000m3 that were necessary to sustain life in these barren hills.

It was later used by Herod as a notorious dungeon, in which he incarcerated and executed many prisoners, including his son – something he seemed to specialise in! The fortress was soon destroyed but eventually renovated by St Sabas (of Mar Saba) in the fifth century, after overcoming the 'evil spirits' that inhabited the site (perhaps as a legacy of Herod's misdeeds?).

Higher up the trail (and a hot sweat if you want to go there – see R28) are the ruins of the sixth-century Monastery of St John, situated on this region's highest top, Jebel Muntar, 524m. Little remains here, but there is a splendid panoramic view extending from Jerusalem to Jordan. It is believed to be the site where the 'scapegoat' was thrown into the abyss in atonement for the sins of Israel.

Biblical reference

'The goat will carry on itself all their sins to a solitary place; and the man shall release it in the desert.'

Leviticus 16: 22, *Holy Bible*, NIV

The trek ends at Mar Saba, with a spectacular view of the monastery clinging to the cliffs of Wadi Qidron, and vying with St George's as one of the most dramatic and inspirational wilderness monastic sites.

Flora and fauna Not a lot to see, though all deserts are, in fact, teaming with life! Ravens fly overhead and small plants and herbs provide minimal nourishment for insects and other small creatures preyed on by birds, lizards and snakes. Additionally, you are likely to see wandering camels and flute-playing or radio-carrying shepherds of the Ja'haleen tribe, and you may also notice their wells with their spreading catchment channels to collect any possible rain and funnel it into the waiting cisterns.

Special advice The whole of the area on either side of the road, from about 5km after Nebi Musa, is an Israeli military training area, only normally open at Jewish holidays and weekends. Anyone wishing to enter must phone first, tel: 02 5305 372 or 03 6976 876.

If you are leaving a car, display in it details of the date, your plans and expected time of return. Don't touch any metallic objects you may see along the way, and do carry plenty of water!

Map SPNI map 8, Also refer to map with R14

Map ref Nebi Musa 1910 1328;   Map ref start 1861 1238

Map ref Hyrcania 1848 1252;   Map ref finish Mar Saba 1815 1235

Approach The actual start of the walk is 11.5km S of Nebi Musa, along the road. A vehicle is recommended to reach the drop-off point, past the military camp, which is situated about 5km S of Nebi Musa. The start of the walk is marked by small green and blue trail signs pointing W into the desert. 100m further on, on each side of the road (at the time of writing), there are two 1m cube concrete blocks with crosses on (alt. 60m).

The route Two 4wd tracks leave the road: blue sign to the left, green to the right. Take the green and head NW across the barren, undulating stony desert towards a conical flat-topped hill, which rises prominently in front of the main escarpment. After almost 2km the track rises steeply up its S side, finally zigzagging to the summit, which is the site of Hyrcania – an excellent vantage point, with views E to the Dead Sea. There is some rare shadow amongst its ruined arches, vaults and walls, which is worth taking advantage of on a hot day (45mins from the road, alt. 248m).

From here, go back down the upper zigzags and take a good track generally NW, first beneath an ancient wall (an aqueduct support?) then winding up the hill to meet improving tracks. Continue uphill for about 45mins (2km) from Hyrcania to meet a 'cross-roads', alt. 367m. The road ahead rises steeply to the summit of Mount Muntar, 524m.

Don't despair – our route doesn't go up the hill – that's R28! Instead, turn L and wind SW along the undulating trail, taking short cuts on shepherds' tracks where convenient, to reach a T-junction after another 2km (45mins). Go L, and after 200–300m a small trail goes R towards one of the towers of Mar Saba Monastery, which can now be seen in the distance. Follow this down for 0.5km or so to reach one of the most dramatic viewpoints in Palestine, with this once incredibly remote monastery hanging from the cliffs of Wadi Qidron directly opposite (2½–3hrs from the road).

To reach the monastery, descend steeply, generally SW, into the wadi (which, sad to say, smells unpleasantly of Jerusalem's sewage). Cross the stream with care and ascend steps up the L (S) side of the monastery to reach the road between the two towers. The monastery entrance is also here. If you intend visiting, verify the opening times before going on the trek to avoid disappointment.

Return Unless you are on the Nativity Trail, in which case you will be camping at Mar Saba, it's advisable to pre-arrange for a special taxi to meet you, otherwise it's a long haul out up 5km of steep road to the first village on the outskirts of Bethlehem.

Taxis For Jerusalem, see R23; for Bethlehem, tel: Asha'b Taxi: 02 2742309 or Beit Jala Taxi: 02 274 2629.

Having spent the night camped near the monastery, walkers of the Nativity Trail will now be ready for their last symbolic day (their 10th or 12th) – the trek to Bethlehem, where Jesus was born:

R14 Day 10. Mar Saba to Bethlehem

'The surrounding limestone hills were wild and wind-worn with panoramic views across the Dead Sea to Jordan in the east and to the hilltop fringes of Bethlehem and Jerusalem to the west. It was a joy to spend the afternoon on the breezy tops and in the quiet valleys with only kestrels, buzzards and the occasional flute-playing shepherd for company.'

'The Nativity Trail', Tony Howard, *Adventure Travel Magazine*, Sept 2000

The trail's final day ascends wild desert hills to the hilltop suburbs of Bethlehem. Then it's on through Beit Sahur (the 'Shepherds' fields') to Bethlehem, Manger Square and the Church of the Nativity, on the site where the original journey ended – and the Christian faith began.

Moderate trek: 8–9km, 3–4hrs to the hilltop village of Dar Saleh above Bethlehem, with a climb from 250m to 471m before descending again to about 250m, then climbing up to 600m. About 570m of ascent and 220m of descent in total. Those determined to walk all the way through the suburbs to the Church of the Nativity should add another 6km.

Special interest The ancient wells and water catchment systems, which are still used by Bedouin, are of particular interest. The well of Bir Ali is a perfect example, with collection basins in the channels to stop silt entering and ancient carved stone drinking troughs, as well as a heavy limestone 'cork' to close the cistern. (At the time of writing its Bedouin owners had also sealed it with cement, so that the water would not be taken by others!) The views E over the Dead Sea to Jordan's Mountains of Moab, including Mount Nebo, are superb.

Flora and fauna Birds of prey drift on the thermals. Large herds of camels wander the hills; these, together with the ubiquitous flute-playing Bedouin shepherds and their flocks, give the area a unique timeless appeal in keeping with this last day of a pilgrimage trail commemorating the momentous event that took place in nearby Bethlehem 2000 years ago.

Special advice Though not a long day, these are dry desert hills, so carry sufficient water.

Map SPNI 8

Map ref start Mar Saba 1815 1236; Map ref finish Dar Saleh 1767 1230.

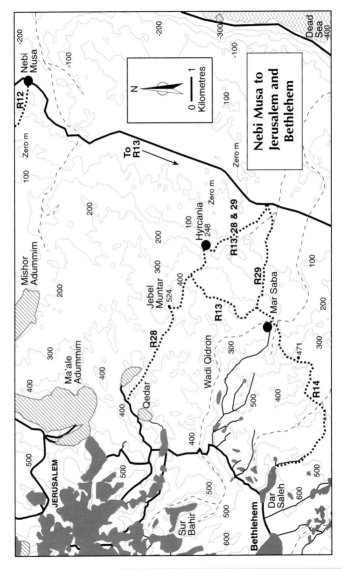

Approach   Those not walking the Nativity Trail will need to take a taxi from Jerusalem or Bethlehem down to Mar Saba.

The route   From the 'Womens' Tower' (the one on the S (R) of the entrance door) a water channel goes S round the hill; follow it to a normally dry riverbed. Cross over and climb the ridge, almost W, to a small top at 364m (almost 1km). Continue W up the ridge, eventually curving S above a steep E-facing drop to reach a summit at 471m, about 2km from Mar Saba.

Follow the ridge top along (ancient graves and splendid panoramic views) generally S for about 1km, before contouring W and descending into a valley on the R (past some ancient threshing areas). Just across the small valley is a white hillside with a well. Cross over to reach the well of Bir Ali, with its catchment channels running up the hillsides and actually round the shoulder of the hill ahead (about 4.5km, approx. 2hrs).

Now, cross the saddle ahead to see the catchment channel going up to the R. Our way goes L, on the L side of a wadi, first following an old wall, then continuing generally S down the valley to meet another wadi (1.5km from Bir Ali).

Follow this up SW then W for about 1.5km to where another wadi enters from the R. Take the path NW up the ridge between the two for another 1.5km. Eventually, it passes below a tell with cave dwellings before passing an olive grove and climbing steeply up to Dar Saleh, reaching it at the mosque.

If you are feeling fit, follow the road W into Beit Sahur (the 'Shepherds' fields') and Bethlehem, otherwise enjoy the ride down to Manger Square and the Church of the Nativity at the end of the Nativity Trail. (For those making their own transport arrangements, go L at the mosque to reach an area of pine trees – named Ghalakto after a Greek monk). There, go R and descend for just over 0.5km to the Bethlehem road to catch a servis.

BETHLEHEM

> *'Bethlehem heralded an eternal message to the world: peace on earth and goodwill toward humankind. Let the year 2000 be a transition for the realisation of the dream of all people – peace, love and fraternity everywhere on earth.'*
>
> Yasser Arafat

Bethlehem is 10km S of Jerusalem, 765m above sea level, on the edge of the Bethlehem Wilderness. An ancient landscape of vineyards, olive

Peter Hall

End of the Nativity Trail
– entering the Grotto of The Nativity, Nativity Church, Bethlehem

trees and villages surrounds the town, which is renowned for its olive wood hand carvings, its mother-of-pearl jewellery, its distinctive and rich embroidery, its friendly people – and, of course, as the place where Christ was born.

Located on an ancient caravan route, Bethlehem has always been a mosaic of many cultures. Not only pilgrims but also numerous foreign rulers have left their trace on the town. Walking through Bethlehem's Old City is like reading a book about history. Canaanite, Byzantine, Arab, Islamic, Persian, Crusader, Turkish and British cultures all influenced traditions and architectural styles. In recent times European religious architecture merged with the Palestinian style to form a precious and challenging contemporary heritage.

The sixth-century Church of the Nativity, parts of which date to the church built by St Helena in 334AD, is one of the oldest complete churches in Christendom and almost indisputably marks the site of Jesus' birth. In 135AD, Emperor Hadrian ordered a pagan temple to be built over the Cave of the Nativity in order to wipe it out. When the Roman empire became Christian, and Helena, wife of Constantine, ordered that a church be built over the spot, the cave was found to have been preserved underneath the pagan temple. Throughout later historical periods, the sanctity of the place was respected. Bethlehem is a Palestinian town of prime importance, though with a minority of Christians amongst its predominantly Muslim population, for whom Jesus is an important Prophet.

Some biblical references

Death of Rachel	Genesis 35: 16–19
Ruth (King David's great-grandmother)	The book of Ruth
David anointed king	1 Samuel 16: 1 and 6–13
David and Jonathan	1 Samuel 18–20
The birth of Jesus	Luke 2: 1–20

For map and further information on Bethlehem see R31.

OTHER ROUTES

Returning north, to Lower Galilee, we start once again back at Mount Tabor with an enjoyable and relaxing circumnavigation of its summit.

R15 Mount Tabor Circuit

'Esdraelon is seen to the greatest advantage, not from the summit, but from a projecting terrace some four hundred feet above Deburieh. It appears like one vast carpet thrown back to the hills.... In variety of patterns and richness of colours, it is not equalled by anything in this country. Both the Mediterranean and the Lake of Tiberias are visible from a point near the summit, the former to the north-west, and the latter on the north-east'

The Land and the Book, W. M. Thomson, 1876

A wonderful woodland stroll with unique panoramas around a site that is not only significant to Christianity but also dates back into pre-history. Tabor was also the setting for numerous important battles over the last three millennia. Though the basilica and other monastic buildings are often within view, the route quickly takes the walker 'far from the madding crowds'.

Easy walk: 2km. Allow 1hr to enjoy the 'bird's-eye' panoramic view and the historical and spiritual ambience of this forest trail. Ascents and descents are minimal, as the path effectively contours this 562m mountain just below its summit.

Special interest From viewpoints on the walk or from the ruins around to basilica it is possible to see Mount Hermon far to the N, beneath which is the location of the Battle of the Horns of Hittin. Lower still, and to the NE, is the Sea of Galilee in its hollow, but visible on a clear day. The Mediterranean is also supposed to be visible to the W (though it was too hazy to see either both times we were there). Looking S, the hills of biblical Gilboa rise beyond the plain of Jezreel. Also see R2.

Some biblical references, Flora and fauna, Special advice See R2.

Map SPNI 3
Map ref Mt Tabor 1867 2325
Also refer to map with R2

Approach By bus from Nazareth, changing at Afulla for the infrequent connection which will bring you to the car park at the bottom of the mountain. Better to take a special taxi, which, if you wish, will drive you all the way to top. (Or you can get a shuttle-taxi up from the car park if you arrive by other transport.)

If you take the road up, just before the top the L fork goes to the Greek church. The R goes though a quite impressive arch, originally part of Melek el-Adel's 12th-century fortress wall but restored in 1868. The car park for the Franciscan church is 200m beyond. (There is also a far nicer way up from the car park – see R2, first day of the Nativity Trail.)

The route From the summit car park (before or after visiting the church) walk back down the road through Melek el Adel's Gate of the Winds. 50m beyond, a black trail marker and wooden sign indicate a trail going L (S) into the trees.

Follow it, descending slightly at first, then levelling out as it passes below the church (occasionally glimpsed above, through the foliage).

Mary Hartley

The watery plain of Jezreel is visible over 400m below to the S. Continue contouring then rising a little past a cave as you circumnavigate the mountain in an anti-clockwise direction. Occasional clearings provide more superb views, this time N, across the rolling land of Galilee 300m below to Mount Hermon in the far distance.

The path continues round, passing another cave and ruins then eventually following a wall (behind which is the road to the Greek church). After crossing the road, the trail arrives almost immediately at the starting point near the Gate of the Winds.

Giant fennel

Return Either arrange to be met by special taxi to take you to the car park at the bottom or walk back down the road, taking shortcuts to eliminate the zigzags (1km, less than ½hr). Here, there are small cafés, toilets, souvenir stalls and opportunities to get a lift back to Nazareth. It would also, of course, be possible (and pleasant) to reverse R2 down to the car park.

Moving S, you should not miss the opportunity to spend at least half a day in the old Palestinian town of Nablus. Better still, why not also have a night there?

NABLUS

The biblical Shechem, Nablus had been a well-established Canaanite town since 1900BC. It was here that Abraham entered the land of Canaan and Jacob bought land. It was here also that Joseph was buried. The Samaritans, who live on Mount Gerizim directly above the town, believe it is the place where Abraham prepared to sacrifice his son, Isaac, rather than in Jerusalem. A Roman colony, Neapolis, was built here following the First Jewish Revolt in 66–73BC (hence the name Nablus). Early in the Christian era, Christianity became well established here. Nablus was also the scene of one of the most moving and meaningful stories in the gospel, the meeting of Jesus with a Samaritan woman at the well at Shechem. Since the capture of the city by the Arabs in 636AD, Nablus has been a thriving Arab town, and remains so today.

Some biblical references

Abraham and Isaac	Genesis 22: 1–14
Land bought by Jacob	Genesis 33: 18–20
Burial of Joseph	Joshua 24: 32
Jesus meets a Samaritan woman	John 4: 5–30

R16 Exploring Nablus

'The streets of Nablus are narrow, many are vaulted over, and in winter the brooks frequently overflow and rush over the pavements with a loud noise; then, of course, it is difficult to traverse them. But the mulberry, orange, and pomegranate grow amongst the houses, scenting the air, and thousands of birds sing in the town itself as well as in the beautiful valley. From the sides of Ebal and Gerizim fall the purest and sweetest springs in fresh rills, and the inmates of Nablus have every physical advantage and beauty in their city'

Palestine Past and Present, L. Valentine, circa 1919

Nablus is unique. Explore it, and enjoy it! Cradled between the Samaritan's two holiest mountains – Gerizim and Ebal – Nablus is, like Bethlehem and Ramallah, in Zone A, under total Palestinian control. Just minutes from its typically bustling Arabic city centre are the ancient buildings, winding alleyways and arched tunnel-like passages of the old town or casbah.

Easy walk: 2–3km. Allow half a day to enjoy the casbah and its unique atmosphere even though you are rarely more than 10mins walk from the main bus and servis station.

Special advice Dress modestly and with respect for the traditions of the Palestinian people – particularly if you intend visiting any of the holy sites. Both sexes can use the Turkish Baths, where you can also have coffee and kanafe (a sticky, sweet concoction made from white cheese, semolina and honey) and smoke the 'hubble-bubble' whilst waiting. There are special times for women – Tuesday is women's day at the Hammam as-Shifa, but you may be able to make special arrangements if it's quiet. The cost is around 15NIS plus another 15NIS for an invigorating massage.

Special interest Nablus has all the fascination of the 'old' Middle East, with its markets, mosques, churches and ancient casbah. There you will find the Turkish Baths (see notes preceding R10), soap and spice makers and old palaces – even the food, such as kanafe, is special! Not to be missed (though many do!).

Some biblical references See above.

Map information Most travel guides have maps of 'down town' Nablus. None that we know of has adequate maps of the maze of passages in the casbah – not even the Tourist Office near Midan Al Hussein Square and clock tower.

Approach Nablus is about 50km N of Jerusalem, via Ramallah. Servis taxis shuttle constantly between the towns; it's about 6NIS to Ramallah then another 9NIS to Nablus. The whole journey normally takes about 1–1½hrs.

The route Well, to be honest, there isn't one really – it's up to you to explore at will, probably getting lost in the maze of alleyways, but inevitably meeting local people and making your own discoveries along the way!

We definitely recommend it, so here's a few tips: assuming you arrive at the bus/servis station in the NW of town, walk SE to find the Midan

Peter Hall

In the casbah of old Nablus

al Hussein circle, about 5mins away. Continue in the same general direction onto the first of the two main E–W streets, Sharia Jamaa'a al Kabir. A short way E is the Midan al Manara Square with its clock tower. Crossing the S side of the square is Sharia al Nasr.

Between these two streets, and S and W of them, is the casbah. On Al Nasr Street you will find Al Badr soap factory on the L. A little further on up an alley is the semi-ruined Palace of Qasr Touqan. Further on again along Al Nasr Street is the wonderful old Hammam as Shifa (Turkish Baths).

A second Hammam, Al Hana Assumara, will be found S through the alleyways of the casbah, up the next street on the L. Near here, in the maze of passages, is another soap factory and a spice warehouse, both in ancient buildings and definitely worth a visit. The museum is a few minutes SE of Manara Square (entry 3NIS) and deals informatively with life in the casbah.

Our best advise is to hire a local Palestinian guide who will take you through the living heart of the old Nablus, and explain its history and the changes that have happened both in the distant and recent past. An informative visit to the refugee camps can also be arranged.

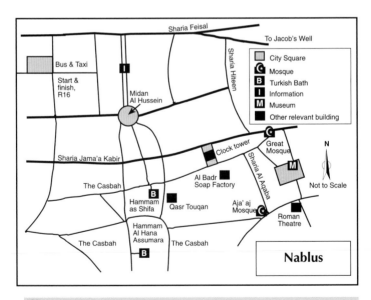

Alternative Tours in Nablus Try 'A Peek into Palestine', tours with a unique insight into Nablus. Contact: Nazar Kamal, tel: 052 685578, or Neta Golan, 02 234378, e-mail: neta_golan@hotmail.com

Accommodation Al Qasr Hotel, tel: 09 2385444. Al Yasmeen Hostel/Motel, Tel: 09 2333555, also 09 2384055; Fax: 09 233 3666. E-mail yasmeen@p-ol.com Website: www.alyasmeen.com

Public transport Buses and servis taxis leave frequently from the bus station for most destinations

Taxis Al I'ttimad, tel: 092371439; Al Madina, tel: 09 2373501

Whilst in the Nablus area it is also worth visiting:

JACOB'S WELL
Believed to be on the land bought by Jacob, where Jesus met the Samaritan woman, the 35m deep well is next to a Greek Orthodox church on the site of previous Byzantine and Crusader churches.

MOUNT GERIZIM
2hrs walk uphill from Nablus (or NIS25 one way) this mountain is claimed by the Samaritans to be Mount Moriah (as against the Orthodox Jewish site of the 'Temple Mount'). From its soil, God is supposed to have made Adam. There is a museum in the village and ruins of a second-century temple nearby.

SEBASTIA
Inhabited from about 4000BC, Sebastia eventually gained fame as King Omri's capital and is now one of the largest archaeological sites in Palestine.

Travelling S down Palestine's West Bank, the rolling hills of Nablus descend gently W towards the coast. Though Israeli settlements and bypass roads seem inescapable there are still valleys that retain the quiet, rural ambience of Palestine, for example:

R17 Wadi Zerqa and Wadi Natuf

A very pleasant walk in the heart of traditional Palestinian land through verdant Wadi Zerqa with its ancient terraces down to the prehistoric Shuqba Cave and the wilder Wadi Natuf.

Easy Walk: 12km. About 5hrs. Descending from 300m to 100m (with a rise of 30m at half way to visit Shuqba Cave). The walk could be

continued down the wadi for another 5km, almost to the outer suburbs of Tel Aviv.

Special interest It's not just the being there, it's the 'getting there'! Your journey there and back through classical rural Palestine will give you an insight into part of the current Middle East situation. Visually incongruous 'settlements' are still being built. The bypass roads that are being created to connect them scar the land. Both impose themselves on the original Palestinian communities. Though in the midst of this confusion of cultures, the walk we have chosen takes you first through a valley with traditional Palestinian terraced agriculture on its ancient hillsides. Next, it passes the Shuqba Cave (see R18), a very important prehistoric site dating back around 500,000 years, and finally through the much more open, wilder terrain of Wadi Natuf. An enjoyable walk and a fascinating day with a glimpse of Palestine old and new.

Flora and fauna Springtime would be really be the time to walk these valleys, when the area is full of wild flowers and nature is at its richest. We walked the valley in autumn when the hills were dry, but even then, due to the Blue Springs of Ain Zerqa, the upper valley was still fertile. Lower down, wild giant fennel filled the valley and aromatic herbs scented the air. There were carob trees and fig trees, grapevines, olive trees and blackberry bushes burdened with fruit. Spears of white flowered wild Sea Squill thrust from the dry earth, and numerous other autumn flowering plants spread patches of blue and yellow along the wadi. Birdlife was also still evident in the autumn, as the springs provide year-round water (we noted woodpeckers, flocks of quail, and other small birds). It is also the time of the olive harvest, after the first rains which usually fall in late October. Why not join in this happy communal activity!

Special advice As much as possible, avoid walking in the rocky wadi bed which can be slow going. When the path disappears from one bank, it usually re-emerges as directly as possible on the other. When you get near to the roads (midway and at the end of the walk) it is advisable to leave the riverbed: the villagers put their rubbish there as there is no waste disposal service.

Map SOIS 8-111

Map ref start 1594 1553;   Map ref Shuqba 1542 1544

Map ref finish 1520 1512   Also refer to Map with R18

Approach Abud (on Road 46, off Road 60, which leads N from Ramallah) is one of the nearest Palestinian villages to the start. There are two turn-offs for Ain Zerqa (the Blue Spring), which is where the walk begins: they are about 8km and 5km before reaching Abud (about 17 and 20km from Route 60 along Route 46).

A much more interesting way if you take a 'special' or have a car is to take the road NW from Ramallah past the villages of Ain Qinya and Ras Karkar, with their ancient springs and 'castle', then wind over the hill down to the car park at Ain Zerqa. The turn-off for the spring is 3km NW of Beitillu at a hairpin bend in the valley bottom (or about 5km from Road 46 if you are coming the other way). From the turn-off a driveable dirt road goes to a large parking area near a spring. There is a Palestinian farmhouse nearby, nestled amongst the greenery.

The route It couldn't be easier – 'follow the wadi' would actually suffice, but a few tips along the way should add to its interest.

Cross the little stream to the R bank and walk down past a pool before crossing back L. Continue down the wadi picking the best paths. At the confluence with the next wadi, follow paths R, downstream, passing by olive groves and orchards with row upon row of ancient terracing for vines and other crops on the hillside above. Cross the wadi as and when necessary.

About 1hr from the start (just over 3km) another wadi enters from the R. Turn L and continue downstream passing a well before reaching a spring on the L bank, about 1km from the wadi junction. The spring flows into old carved stone basins beneath a fern-festooned

Mary Hartley

Sea Squill

123

overhang. The Palestinian village visible on the skyline of the high hill to the N is Deir abu Masha'l.

Continue down the wadi, heading generally SW for 1km, to a more open area beyond the trees, where you may well find a Bedouin camp. 1km further on, the wadi meets the road coming down from Shuqba (see R18). Sadly the last bit of the riverbed is used as a rubbish tip – avoid it by traversing the hillside above to the R (N) to reach the road almost level with Shuqba Cave (alt. 220m; about 7km from the start).

Wadi Zerqa ends here and becomes Wadi Natuf, giving its name to the prehistoric Natufian culture, a Pleistocene period which was previously unknown until fossils and tools were found in the Shuqba Cave – the huge gaping hole just ahead on the R bank of the wadi. To reach the spectacular cave, rise gently across the hillside on paths (the reverse of the 'return' for R18). From the cave, descend gently to regain the wadi just beyond the distant olive grove. Follow the dry river down (mostly on the L bank) through the wild and open valley to reach another isolated olive grove in about ½hr. Just beyond is the first dramatic view of the village of Na'alin, with its tall minaret piercing the skyline.

A little further on the trail passes by a Bedouin camp beyond which the approach to the village is once again full of garbage. Leave the wadi and walk R through trees to the road.

Return Here's the potentially tricky bit! No problem if you came with two cars – just leave one at each end of the walk. Otherwise, you have some decisions to make: either walk 1km L up to the village of Na'alin and get a servis or special taxi via Qibya to Shuqba, Abud and the start of the walk at Ain Zerqa (or directly back to Ramallah); or stay where you are and try hitching! We (four of us) got a lift immediately on a tractor and trailer to Qibya, then continued in a van to Shuqba, then in a 'special' to Ain Zerqa where our car was, and where we were treated to tea by the local farmer!

Taxis (Ramallah) Al Bireh, tel: 02 2952956; Darwish, tel: 02 2956150

The previous route passes by a gaping cavern, which is also worth a special visit if you are in the area and have a little time to spare:

R18 The Shuqba Cave

A spectacular cave chamber with two natural 'chimneys' or skylights in its huge domed roof. There are also some minor chambers and a 'side-entrance'. Well worth a visit for the rock scenery as well as for its interest as an important prehistoric site.

Despite its proximity to a road in an area where settlements tend to dominate the landscape, the Shuqba Cave is in a location where 'civilisation' is hidden from view; it is easy to sit in its shadow and imagine oneself back in a land where rhinos roamed!

Easy walk and cave: just over 1km there and back. Allow 1hr for the trip and to appreciate the spectacular cave chamber. The cave is about 30m above the wadi, at an altitude of about 250m.

Special interest The cave is an Upper and Epi-Palaeolithic site possibly dating back 40,000 years. Situated in the valley of Wadi Natuf, it is the site after which the Epi-Palaeolithic Natufian culture was named, as human tools of this period were previously unknown to archaeologists, for example crescent-shaped and sickle-blade flint tools and pointed bone tools and awls. Natufian human burials were found in the cave

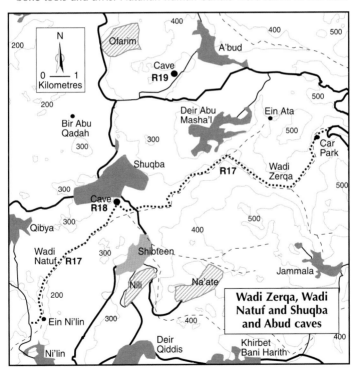

Wadi Zerqa, Wadi Natuf and Shuqba and Abud caves

as well as remains of cattle, deer and gazelle. The older (Upper Palaeolithic) remains include hand axes and blades and remains of hippopotamus and rhinoceros. Flint shards and fossil bones can still be found.

Flora and fauna In the brief walk from the road, we passed by a small olive grove and orchard with figs (September). Okra was growing in a small field; the crop had finished but some of them were left for their seeds for next year's planting. Wild fennel and aromatic herbs grow beneath and on the cliffs. In springtime, flowers are everywhere.

Map SOIS 8-111
Map ref Shuqba Cave 1542 1544

Approach The village of Shuqba is about 20km NW of Ramallah. The easiest approach is to take Road 60 N from Ramallah, towards Nablus, turning L (W) after about 6km, near Bir Zeit, onto Road 46. Follow this for about 20km to Abud then take the minor Road 4460 SW for about 5km to Shuqba. Here turn L and descend for 1km into Wadi Natuf. Just before reaching the bottom, the huge gaping cave mouth will be seen to the R.

The route From the small lay-by either follow Wadi Natuf W (or avoid the litter in the riverbed by walking through the olive grove and

Flax

orchard). Just beyond, zigzag gently up the increasingly rocky hillside to reach the cave, which is about 40m deep and 30m high.

It is well worthwhile scrambling up the side of the cliff (easiest on the left of the cave – Grade 1) to reach the two 'sky-lights' in the roof of the main chamber for a frightening view into the abyss – take care!

Return Either walk back the same way, or simply descend a little before contouring round to reach the road just above the olive grove.

Taxis (Ramallah) see R17.

Whilst in the area, why not visit another cave:

R19 The Abud Cave

Once you have found it (which may not be easy) the comparatively small entrance leads to quite a large main chamber with cave features and some passages that may repay further exploration. The main chamber can be muddy in the winter, but that's what caving is all about!

Easy cave: 1hr is plenty of time to enjoy the view, the 0.5km round-trip and the cave – unless you manage to find some new passages! The cave entrance, which is concealed from view from most aspects, is only about 50m above the road and 200m away at approximately alt. 360m.

Flora and fauna There are bats in the cave, whilst by the roadside verges of this area you may see small prickly haired plants flowering in September. The small yellow flowers are unremarkable, though the many pale green, 3cm long bulbous seed pods are more unusual: if you touch them they 'explode', firing a powerful jet of liquid about 3m into the air (mind your eyes), thus giving rise to their delightful local name, Fuss el Humar – 'Donkey's fart' (more correctly called the Squirting Cucumber).

Special advice To explore this cave you need torches (head torches are best) and, if you are extremely lucky and find some ongoing passages, you may even need some caving gear. (In this case you should also have an experienced caver with you.)

Map SOIS 8-111

Map ref Abud Cave 1556 1576

Also refer to the map with R18

Approach The cave is located just above the old road, which runs SW from Abud to Shuqba about 20km NW of Ramallah. Approach as for

Shuqba Cave, N from Ramallah on Road 60 then W on Road 46 for 20km to Abud.

From Abud centre, take the small road L, which winds down into the valley. 300m below the village, a lane goes R. Pass this and continue down to a small parking space on the R, level with the fourth metal pylon and opposite the end of a wall on the L. (Coming in the other direction, up the road from Shuqba, it's the second roadside pylon.)

The route Scramble diagonally up the hillside in a WSW direction towards a prominent thorny tree exactly on the skyline and about 100m L of a small cliff. If you are lucky you should find the cave entrance in a hollow directly behind the tree. If not, search around – you are close!

Inside the low entrance, the cave abruptly opens out to a main chamber about 30m in diameter and 5–10m high. A central stalagmite, 1–2m thick, supports the roof. A small shaft of light comes through the roof at the far right and (we were told) a narrow cave passage continues for 30–40m from the back of the chamber (not explored by the authors, as we had no torches with us when we visited the cave).

Taxis (Ramallah) see R17.

Other things to do in this area The ancient Palestinian and Ottoman village of Ras Karkar, which is midway between Shuqba and Ramallah, is also worth seeing. There is a castle built in the 18th century by Ibn Samhan with beautifully carved inscriptions and decorative motifs. The views from this high vantage point are excellent.

Still moving S we return to:

Jerusalem

'May those who love you be secure. May there be peace within your walls and security within your citadels.'

Psalm 122: 6–7, *Holy Bible, NIV*

The city is one of the world's most holy and disputed religious cities, sacred to all three monotheistic faiths: Islam, Judaism and Christianity. Its name reputedly originates from the Canaanite word Ur-salem, in which the Aramaic language spoken by Jesus has its roots. Since prehistoric times it has been a holy place, the original Canaanite shrine being destroyed when the Hebrews built the First Temple on the site now dominated by the Dome of the Rock:

Wadi Auja, Day 6 of the Nativity Trail

The monastery of Mar Saba, Day 9 of the Nativity Trail

Climbing the hills between Mar Saba and Bethlehem, Day 10 of the Nativity Trail

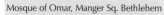
Wadi Khureitun with its prehistoric caves

Mosque of Omar, Manger Sq. Bethlehem

In the market, Bethlehem

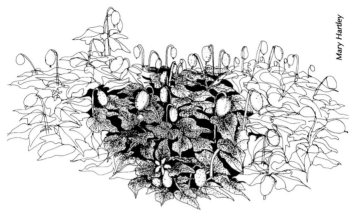

Mary Hartley

Squirting cucumber

Haram Al Sharif – The Noble Sanctuary or Temple Mount

'Glory to the One Who took His Servant for a Journey by night from the Sacred Mosque to the Farthest Mosque whose precincts We did bless.'

The Holy Qur'an, sura 17, verse 1

Known to Jews as Mount Moriah, archaeological evidence suggests that this place was sacred to the original occupants of the land, the Canaanites and Philistines, ancestors of the Palestinians. Interestingly, both the Jewish and Islamic words for God originate from the name of the Canaanite God El, hence the Hebrew 'Elohim' and Arabic 'Allah'.

In the biblical record, it was here that Abraham offered his son, Isaac, in sacrifice to God. Here, the Temple of Solomon, which contained the Holy of Holies and the Ark of the Covenant, was built in 961BC. This Temple was destroyed by the Babylonians in 586BC, but was rebuilt by Zerubbabel in 537–515BC.

Herod rebuilt the Second Temple in 22BC, which Jesus attended regularly on his pilgrimages to the Holy City. It was destroyed by the Romans in 70AD. The Western Wall (Wailing Wall), the most holy place in Judaism, is an exposed stretch of the Herodian retaining wall. After its destruction by the Romans, the Temple platform was neglected until the Arab conquest of Jerusalem, when the Dome of the Rock

(688–692AD) and the Al-Aqsa Mosque (705–715AD) were built. The former is on the supposed site of Mohammed's night journey to heaven on his winged horse, Buraq, where he met Abraham, Moses and Jesus.

Some biblical references

Abraham offers his son in sacrifice to God	Genesis 22: 1–19
The Temple of Solomon	1 Kings 5: 1–18
The presentation of Christ in the Temple	Luke 2: 22–29
Jesus visiting the Temple as a boy	Luke 2: 41–51
Clearing market-stalls from the Temple precincts	Matthew 21: 12–17

R20 Jerusalem Ramparts and Old City Walk

Jerusalem, Al Qods, The Holy City, revered by half of the world's population – it would be unthinkable to omit it! We have picked an amalgam of walks, but for a first visit you would probably do only a part of them, perhaps the Via Dolorosa or a visit to the Wailing Wall, or Western Wall, as it is otherwise known. For those who want an enjoyable day's walk passing through, or with views of, all aspects of the city, this is a must!

Easy walk: 6km. Allow a minimum of 4hrs to enjoy the walk and soak in the atmosphere of the Holy City. If you intend visiting and spending time at the holy sites you will need a full day (at least). The route goes round the whole city wall of Old Jerusalem except the section adjacent to the Haram Al Sharif, which is closed for security reasons. The sections of the walk on the streets of the Old City are well shaded and there are numerous cafés in the Muslim Quarter on both the Via Dolorosa and El Wad Street.

Special interest Here everything is of special interest! Numerous guidebooks are devoted to Jerusalem, but here are some key features. The 4km of Jerusalem's wall were built in the 16th century by Suleiman the Magnificent. From them you will see all of Old Jerusalem – the bustling Damascus Gate, the Dome of the Rock and Al Aqsa Mosque, built 688–693, and the 14th-century Citadel. You will also pass through the Jewish, Muslim, Armenian and Christian Quarters, as well as passing by the Wailing Wall and walking the Via Dolorosa to the Church of the Holy Sepulchre, marking the site of Christ's crucifixion on Golgatha – what more could you want in a day!

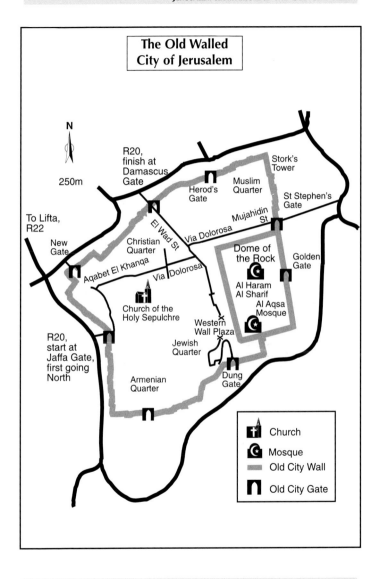

The Old Walled
City of Jerusalem

N

250m

R20,
finish at
Damascus
Gate

Stork's
Tower

Muslim
Quarter

Herod's
Gate

St Stephen's
Gate

Mujahidin St

To Lifta,
R22

New
Gate

Christian
Quarter

El Wad St

Via Dolorosa

Dome of
the Rock

Golden
Gate

Aqabet El Khanqa

Via Dolorosa

Al Haram
Al Sharif

Al Aqsa
Mosque

Church of the
Holy Sepulchre

Western
Wall Plaza

R20,
start at
Jaffa Gate,
first going
North

Jewish
Quarter

Armenian
Quarter

Dung
Gate

Church

Mosque

Old City Wall

Old City Gate

Ethiopian monk drowsing outside the Ethiopian monastery on the roof of the Church of the Holy Sepulchre, the location of Christ's crucifixion

Peter Hall

Some biblical references

St Stephen's Gate: supposed site of martyrdom of Stephen, the first Christian martyr. Acts 7: 44–60

Pools of Bethesda: healing of paralysed man. John 5: 2–9

First Station of the Cross: Jesus is condemned to death. Mark 15: 1–15

Station 2: Chapel of Flagellation and Condemnation. Matthew 27: 27–31 and Mark 15: 16-20

Station 3: Jesus falls for the first time. Hebrews 2: 17–18

Station 4: Jesus meets his mother. Luke 1: 30–33

Station 5: Simon of Cyrene compelled to carry cross. Matthew 27: 32

Station 6: Veronica wipes the sweat from Jesus' face.

Station 7: Jesus falls for the second time. Isaiah 53: 5–6

Station 8: Jesus consoles the women of Jerusalem. Luke 23: 27–28

Station 9: Jesus falls for the third time. Not marked, but contemplated at the entrance to the Holy Sepulchre. 1 Peter 2: 22–24

The remaining stations are all in the Holy Sepulchre Church, built over the old quarry known as Golgotha, which King Herod made a place of public execution. The Roman Catholic chapel at the top of the stairs on the right as you enter the church is where these stations are commemorated:

Station 10: Jesus is stripped of his garments. John 19: 23–24

Station 11: Jesus is nailed to the cross. Luke 23: 33–34

Station 12: Jesus dies on the cross. This is marked in the Greek Orthodox chapel immediately next to the above. The ornate altar is built directly over the site of the crucifixion. Luke 23: 44–46

Station 13: Jesus is taken down from the cross. John 19: 38

Leave the Calvary chapels by the steps at the rear of the Greek Orthodox chapel. At the bottom of the steps (in front of the main entrance to the church) is the slab of stone on which, according to tradition, the body of Jesus was lain.

Station 14: Jesus is laid in the tomb. John 19: 40–41

Known as the Anastasis (resurrection), the site of the tomb of Jesus is covered by a large (and unsightly) aedicule. The aedicule was built fewer than 200 years ago by the Turkish authorities over the site of the original tomb, which was destroyed in the 11th century.

Resurrection of Jesus: John 20: 1–24

Special advice If you intend visiting any holy sites, you should dress discreetly and with respect. One more point – there is an entry fee for the ramparts walk, 15NIS payable at the Jaffa or Damascus Gates and valid for two days. Though you can exit at other places, these are the only entry points to the wall, which is open 9.00 to 16.00 (14.00 Fridays).

Maps There are maps of Jerusalem in all guidebooks, or you can get free maps near the start of this walk at the Jaffa Gate.

The route Enter at the Jaffa Gate (N side). Walk the wall to the Damascus Gate (Bab el Amud). It is best to take a detour below rather then above the gate here to see archaeological layers of the Old City, together with a display of ancient olive presses, etc. Back on top, continue clockwise round to St Stephen's Gate on the E (about 2.5km from the start). The Mount of Olives and Garden of Gethsemane are across the valley to the E.

Descend to enter the typically narrow cobbled Mujahidin Street, which is the start of the Via Dolorosa. Beyond are the Church of St Anne and Pools of Bethesda. Continue a short way to the First Station of the Cross (the courtyards of the Al' Omariyeh School are on the L – site of the Fortress of Antonia). Next, is the Second Station. Nearby is the Convent of the Sisters of Zion and the Lithostratus, the old Roman pavement where Jesus was tried (a must for anyone interested in the Christian story, and also for ancient underground cisterns and the Struthion Pool preserved beneath). Further on down the hill, the Via Dolorosa reaches its junction with El Wad Street. Here, the route turns L at Station 3, then R up the narrow Aqabet El Khanqa at the fourth Station (also depicted above the doorway of a small Armenian Catholic chapel). Station 5 is just beyond – the lintel of a doorway is marked with an inscription and a Roman numeral V. Behind the door is a Franciscan oratory. Next is Station 6, reputed to be on the site of the home of Veronica (a big wooden door with studded metal bands on it bears the Roman numerals VI). 10m further on, up a flight of steps, the Greek Church of the Holy Face and St Veronica can be viewed through a metal door.

Up the hill 75m from the previous station (just above where the Aqabet El Khanqa joins the original main road of Jerusalem, the Cardo, now the Suq Khan ez Zeit), and above a doorway, are the Roman numerals VII. The door is often hidden by market stalls and is usually locked. Behind it are two chapels. This position marks the W boundary of Jerusalem in Jesus' time. From this point onwards, Jesus carried his cross *outside* the city walls. Beyond is Station 8, which is very difficult to find. It is simply a slice of pillar embedded in the street wall and inscribed with the Greek letters *NIKA for* 'Jesus Christ conquers'. Then comes the turning L to the Church of the Holy Sepulchre in which the final Stations of the Cross (9–14) are situated in this site of the crucifixion.

Perhaps you will already have visited the church? If not, you may wish to return to spend some time there another day, as our route continues up through the Christian Quarter without turning off to the church. At the top (Church of St Saviour on R) the street bends L and goes S down Cosa Nova Street to return to the Jaffa Gate. This point is approximately half-way, about 3km from the start.

Here, we regain the wall, this time on the S side of the gate. Back on the ramparts, continue, this time anti-clockwise, past the Citadel with its prominent Muslim minaret built in 1655. The wall now passes between the Dormition Church and the Armenian Quarter, eventually reaching the Dung Gate, where the Dome of the Rock and Al Aqsa Mosque are once again visible. Here, descend and enter the Jewish Quarter before descending steps R down to the Plaza of the Wailing Wall directly below Al Aqsa Mosque (security check point), 2k from the Jaffa Gate.

Peter Hall

Statues in the city wall, Christian Quarter, Jerusalem

Peter Hall

The Citadel and its 17th-century minaret, now commonly known as the Tower of David

Cross the Plaza and pass through a tunnel leading N past a second security check before entering the Muslim Quarter at El Wad Street. Go N up this to reach the Damascus Gate.

The next route, a pilgrim's way, takes you to, or within view of, more world famous religious sites:

R21 The Palm Sunday Walk

'There is the view from the Mount of Olives, down twenty miles of desert hill-tops to the deep blue waters [of the Dead Sea], with the wall of Moab glowing on the further side like burnished copper, and staining the blue sea red with its light'
The Historical Geography of the Holy Land, George Adam Smith, 1894

The walk follows the route that Jesus took to Jerusalem, now celebrated on Palm Sunday. As much a Christian pilgrimage as a walk, though there is certainty enough uphill to get you sweating on a hot day! There are also some excellent classical views W from the top of the Mount of Olives over Wadi Qidron to the walls, domes, minarets and modern skyline of Jerusalem.

Easy walk. 4km. Allow at least 3hrs to do the walk and visit some sites. You could easily spend much longer. Perhaps 150m of ascent and descent. There are places for drinks and snacks along the way.

Special interest The route commences in Bethany, often frequented by Jesus and where he was anointed before the Last Supper. A modern Franciscan church designed by Antonio Barluzzi lies close to the supposed site of Lazarus' Tomb, whose original rock-cut walls are obscured by a Crusader-built chamber.

From the tomb where Jesus raised Lazarus from the dead to the amazement of the people and the wrath of the Jewish Sanhedrin, the route climbs up to Bethphage on the E slopes of the Mount of Olives. Monasteries and convents of differing denominations mark the place where he mounted the donkey.

The route continues to the Mount of Olives and the Pater Noster Church, with its interesting collection of the Lord's Prayer in many different languages. The Mosque of Ascension is nearby. From here there is a magnificent view of the Old City of Jerusalem, dominated by the golden glow of the Dome of the Rock – Islam's third holiest shrine, on the Haram al Sharif or Noble Sanctuary.

The walk then descends to the Garden of Gethsemane past the Jewish Cemetery, the Church of Dominus Flavit (where Jesus wept over the city) and the Russian Church of Mary Magdalene. The Church of all Nations (Basilica of the Agony) is alongside, and the Tomb of Mary and The Grotto where Judas gave Christ the 'kiss of death' are opposite. The walk enters the Old City at St Stephen's Gate, site of the first Christian martyrdom, then goes via the first section of the Via Dolorosa to the Third Station of the Cross before exiting up El Wad Street to the Damascus Gate. Plenty to meditate on!

Some biblical references

Bethany. Al-Azariyya. (The Arabic name is derived from Lazarus.) Where Jesus' friends and followers Mary, Martha and Lazarus lived.

Jesus and his disciples in Bethany — Mark 10: 38–42

Jesus makes his triumphant entry into Jerusalem — Mark 11: 11–12

Jesus anointed by Mary — Mark 14: 3–9

Jesus raises Lazarus from the dead. — John 11: 17–44

Bethphage From here, Jesus makes his triumphal entry into the city, an event celebrated as Palm Sunday. — Luke 19: 28–36 and Mark 11: 1–11

Mount of Olives Since about 1500BC, this has been a place of burial, and continues so to this day. It is believed that this is the place where the final judgment of God will take place. — Joel 3: 2 and Zechariah 14: 4

It was this hill that King David crossed when his life was threatened by his son, Absalom. — 2 Samuel 15: 13–18 and 30–37

For Christians, the Mount of Olives is remembered mostly as the place where Jesus often sat with his disciples and taught them. — Mark 13: 3–13

The Church of the Pater Noster is nearby, where tradition has it that Jesus taught his disciples the Lord's Prayer. — Mathew 6: 5–15

Jesus enters the city of Jerusalem on Palm Sunday. — Luke 19: 37–44

Jesus arrested in the Garden of Gethsemane. — Mark 14: 26–50

There are several other important Christian and Muslim pilgrimage sites on the Mount of Olives:

King David leaves the city after Absalom's revolt. — 2 Samuel 15: 24–30

The Mosque and Chapel of the Ascension mark the supposed site of Jesus' ascension into heaven. — Acts 1: 6–12

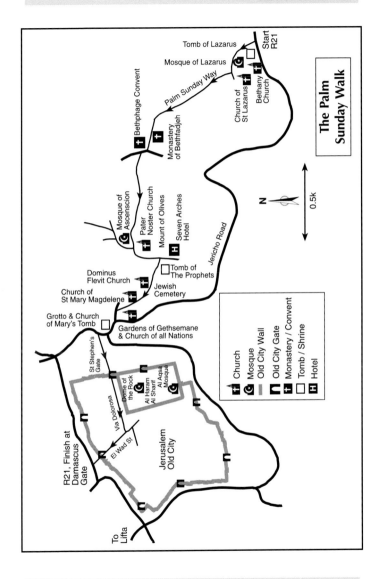

The Palm Sunday Walk

Tomb of Lazarus
Start R21
Mosque of Lazarus
Palm Sunday Way
Church of St Lazarus
Bethany Church
Bethphage Convent
Monastery of Bethfadjeh
N
0.5k
Mosque of Ascenscion
Pater Noster Church
Mount of Olives
Seven Arches Hotel
Jericho Road
Dominus Flevit Church
Tomb of The Prophets
Church of St Mary Magdelene
Jewish Cemetery
Grotto & Church of Mary's Tomb
Gardens of Gethsemane & Church of all Nations
St Stephen's Gate
Dome of the Rock
Al Haram Al Sharif
Al Aqsa Mosque
Via Dolorosa
El Wad St
R21, Finish at Damascus Gate
Jerusalem Old City
To Lifta

Church
Mosque
Old City Wall
Old City Gate
Monastery / Convent
Tomb / Shrine
Hotel

Peter Hall

Mosque and church at the site of the Tomb of Lazarus, Bethany

The Church of Dominus Flevit marks the site where Jesus wept over the city of Jerusalem.   Luke 19: 41–44

Nearby is the Russian Church of Mary Magdalene. At the foot of the slope, in the Qidron Valley, are the Tomb of Mary and Cave of the Olive Press, the Garden of Gethsemane and the Church of All Nations.
  Mark 14: 32–50,
  Luke 22: 39–54 and
Mathew 26: 36–56

Visible from the Mount of Olives, across the Qidron Valley, is the Dome of the Rock, on the Haram Al Sharif (see R20). From the foot of the Mount of Olives, the walk finishes along the first section of the Via Dolorosa (see R20).

Flora and fauna In springtime, there are flowers in abundance, but the gardens at the Church of Bethany by the Tomb of Lazarus are pleasant at any time of year, and the hillside churches on the Mount of Olives are in an idyllic and peaceful location despite their proximity to the city. Pine, olive and Cypress trees surround their tranquil gardens. Some of the olive trees in the Garden of Gethsemane are reputed to originate from the time of Christ and were a 'silent witness to His agony'.

Special advice Dress modestly and with respect for the holy sites you will be visiting. Check the numerous guidebooks for opening times of the various churches and other sites.

Maps Not all guidebooks have maps going beyond (E) of the Mount of Olives, but look for the 'Map of Jerusalem and Bethlehem', Arab Hotel Association. Tel: 02 6281805. Web: www.palestinehotels.com

Approach Take a 'special' or' 'servis' taxi up from E of the Damascus Gate (2.5NIS for a 'servis') to Izariyya (Al -Azariyya). Ask for the Tomb (Maqam) of Lazarus.

The route The Tomb of Lazarus is behind the Bethany Church, beneath the mosque. From the Tomb, go up the road and turn immediately R along a quiet lane. Go up this steeply for a little more then 0.5km, when it turns into a rough track. This continues up between high monastery walls for 0.25km, reaching a road just after passing the entrance to the Greek Orthodox Monastery of Bethfadjeh. Here is the Franciscan Covent of Bethphage. Both are close to the spot where tradition says that Jesus mounted a donkey to make his triumphal entry into Jerusalem on the first Palm Sunday.

Turn R onto the road, then immediately L and up steeply up again for 0.5km to reach the top of the Mount of Olives and the Pater Noster

Church on the L. (Up the road a short way to the R, is the Mosque of the Ascension.)

Go down L, to arrive above the W slope of the Mount of Olives with its famous panoramic view of Jerusalem. (The Seven Arches Hotel is just a little further on). Before reaching the hotel, steps lead down R to a narrow lane that descends steeply towards Gethsemane. On the L are the Tombs of the Prophets, Haggai, Zacharia and Malachai. Further down, also on the L, is the Jewish cemetery, as it is believed that this is the site of the Resurrection of the Dead on the Day of Judgment.

On the R side of the lane are the idyllic churches of Dominus Flavit and Mary Magdalene, with its distinctive golden Russian domes. At the bottom of the hill are the Garden of Gethsemane and the All Nations Church. The Church of Mary's Tomb is almost opposite, as is the Grotto where Jesus was betrayed by Judas.

From here, it's about 0.25km to the city. Head R up the busy road that rises out of the Qidron Valley. Another road goes L immediately. Ignore this and take the next L up a small road, directly to St Stephen's Gate (the Lion's Gate – identified by the carved lions on its wall). Once through the gate you are on Mujahidin Street, the start of the Via Dolorosa. Follow it for 0.25km to the Third Station of the Cross, where it meets El Wad Street Turn R up El Wad Street to reach the Damascus Gate after another 0.25km.

On the other side of Jerusalem, NW of the Damascus Gate, is another site well worth visiting to understand more recent, but equally turbulent and tragic, Middle East history:

R22 Exploring Lifta

A short walk amongst the ruins of a once uniquely beautiful Palestinian village that now stands abandoned in olive groves and gardens above its spring and pool, bearing silent witness to the occupation of 1948. A visit is essential in understanding something of the current Palestinian situation. It is also easy to imagine what Palestine would have been like in biblical times with its vegetable gardens and orchards of figs, pomegranates, almonds and olives, though the houses of Lifta are of very fine construction, being the homes of stonemasons.

Easy walk. 1km round-trip with about 100m of steep descent and ascent. Allow 1hr or so to explore the ruins with their excellent stonemasonry, abandoned olive press, gardens and other artefacts.

Special interest In 1948, the British Mandate ended and Israel declared Independence. At that time the population of Lifta was around 2500, with shops, schools, a mosque and a coffee-house, which was attacked on the 28th December 1948, killing six of its patrons and wounding seven others. Following this and repeated terrorist action by the Haganah, the IZL and the Stern Gang, which included killing the head of the village, the occupants fled.

Previously, relationships between local Jews and Arabs had been amicable: a Lifta woman said,

> *'We were neighbours who complemented each other. There was little competition. On Saturdays, Jews and Arabs would mingle in the valley market...'.*

Flora and fauna It seems almost irrelevant to talk about 'nature' in this sad place even though it is now, ironically, an Israeli nature reserve. Nevertheless the village of Lifta is in a beautiful valley, and its once well-tended terraces are rich in flora and obviously home to many birds and other creatures. The spring and pool are places for quiet contemplation. (On Fridays, the nearby Jewish communities hold prayer meetings there to establish its Jewish identity.)

Map SPNI 8

Map ref Lifta 1688 1334

Ruins of once beautiful Palestinian homes in Lifta, in the suburbs of Jerusalem

Approach From the Old City of Jerusalem, take the Jaffa Road out NW for about 3.5km (taxi or bus) towards Tel Aviv, as far as Rumeima. There, turn R and then L as the road contours above the deep valley of Lifta. Park a short way down the dirt track.

The route Couldn't be simpler – simply walk down the steep rough track to the ruins and spring, which can be seen below. Explore the area at your will.

Moving back to the NE suburbs of Jerusalem brings you to one of the wildest and most spectacular valleys in Palestine:

R23 Wadi Qelt

> *'Even though I walk through the valley of the Shallow of Death, I will fear no evil'*
>
> 23rd Psalm, *Holy Bible, NIV*

Yes, folks, this is it! And a great place it is too – wild and beautiful with ever changing scenery, rich in wildlife, steeped in history! Walking the valley (or part of it) is a 'must'.

Serious trek. About 20km (10hrs) to St George's Monastery. 25km (12hrs) to Jericho.

Peter Hall

The route descends from 640m to about minus 100m at St George's, or to minus 250m at Jericho. This is a long, hard trek demanding stamina, route-finding ability and confidence to scramble across sections of Grade 1 and 2 polished limestone. Many prefer to do the route over 2 days (see R24 and R25).

After rain it is possible to include a section of the canyon with waterfalls and pools, necessitating swimming – but this will add time.

Special interest This route down a side-fault of the Rift Valley is packed with interest. At times the valley is a chasm or

Old millstones

gorge cut deep into the limestone; occasionally it opens out to gentler terrain. There are springs and oases along the way, third- and fifth-century monasteries, Bedouin camps and even a café at Ain Fawwar. Aqueducts ancient and modern (some dating back over 2000 years to take water to Herod's Temple) carry water down the lower valley and are a delight to follow.

Some biblical references See notes on Wadi Qelt and St George's Monastery preceding R12.

Flora and fauna Wadi Qelt is a nature reserve and International Birdlife Area. Descending, as it does, through three ecosystems and being, for the most part, a linear oasis of greenery due to the constant inflow of water from springs, the valley is home to a great variety of wildlife. During our one-day trek down its full length, we saw a fox, numerous rock hyrax, many lizards and the remains of a porcupine; there were also falcons and their favourite prey, the ubiquitous pigeons, as well as quail, Tristram's Grackles, a kingfisher, an eagle being mobbed by ravens and many other birds. There were also frogs, crabs and fish (some quite large) in the pools and aqueducts, above which bright red and turquoise dragonflies hovered.

The riverbed is, at times, choked with thick beds of mint, buzzing with insects, or tall bamboo-like fragmites reeds which (if our experience in Jordan is anything to go by) are home to snakes such as vipers, so tread carefully! There are also carob trees with their autumn fruit, and tall Cypress trees rise around the monasteries. Other bushes, flowers and plants take full advantage of the permanent stream.

Special advice Like all deep valleys in the region, Wadi Qelt will flash flood after rain. Remember it may well not be raining where you are, but back in the hills of Jerusalem a downfall of rain can send a torrent down the valley. If there's a chance of rain, don't go in the upper canyons.

Finally, the complete walk of this valley in one day from Jerusalem to Jericho should not be attempted on unduly hot days – if it's hot in the Jerusalem hills it will be even hotter, maybe even 10°C more, in Jericho! Also, it's a long way. For maximum enjoyment, our advice is to take two days, which allows more time to visit the various sites along the way – refreshing waterfalls, ancient monasteries and so on (see R24 and R25). Carry adequate clothes to dress decently if you intend entering St George's Monastery.

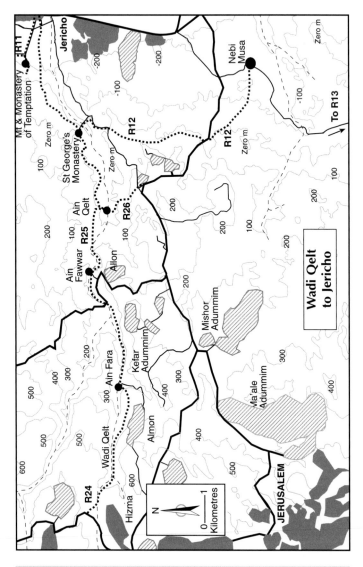

Wadi Qelt to Jericho

Map SPNI 8
Map ref start (Hizma) 1755 1383; Map ref start (alternative) 1755 1390; Map ref finish (St George's) 1890 1390; Map ref finish (Jericho) 1935 1404

Approach The route starts at the Palestinian village of Hizma, 8km NE of Jerusalem Old City (about 13km by road). Either go by special taxi or take a couple of servis: first towards Ramallah, getting off after about 8km by the petrol station at Beit Hanina, then heading E for about 5km to Hizma.

Alternatively, instead of going into Hizma, go down the bypass road just to its N. Start the walk 200m up the road beyond the wide bed of the valley (Wadi Qelt) at some Megalithic mounds.

The route See R24 and R25.

Return From St George's, take the paved track over the bridge and up the hill to the S, reaching the road after 5mins or so, where there are souvenir and drink stalls. Here, you may be lucky in catching a lift with a tour bus. Better to arrange beforehand to be met, or you could phone for a taxi, as mobile phones work at this point.

From Jericho, you can take a bus or servis back to Jerusalem – or why not book in a hotel and stay the night – you deserve it!

Accommodation and transport See notes on Jericho preceding R12. Alternatively you could get a special taxi from Jerusalem:

Abdo, tel: 02 6283281   Aqsa, tel: 02 6273003
Beit Hanina, tel: 02 5855777   Imperial, tel: 02 6282504
Itihad, tel: 02 6286941   Mount of Olives, tel: 02 6272777
Descending the wadi in two days, the first section is (of course):

R24 Upper Wadi Qelt

'The heat became insufferable and the wilderness seemed to close in on me. The air was hot and still. The khaki rocks flung back the sun like the sides of a furnace. Soon there was but little green to be seen. Black goats were grazing on tufts of coarse grass, which grew in the cracks of the rock. Turning a corner, I almost ran into a herd of them. They scattered and leaping to the rocks, their long ears flapping, turned to watch me go by like angry, bearded old men.

Once I met a shepherd painfully climbing the hill, leading his sheep, talking to them all the time, and on his shoulder he carried a lamb, holding it by the four legs as in pictures of the good Shepherd...'

                              In the Steps of the Master, H. V. Morton, 1934

The upper part of Wadi Qelt is wild and wonderful, only opening out into the barren hills of the desert for the last 1km or so before the spring of Ain Fawar. Its descent is amongst the most adventurous in this guide.

Serious trek. 10km. Allow 4–6hrs. Descending from 640m at Hizma to 300m at Ain Fawwar. Some scrambling on Grade 1 and 2 rock.

Special interest If you take the alternative start from the bypass road just N of the Palestinian village of Hizma, there are some rock structures dating to the Megalithic Period. Lower down the canyon, at the springs of Ain Fara are the remains of the Orthodox monastery founded by Chariton in 275AD when he settled there in a robber's cave. Unfortunately for him, his disciples, denying him his search for solitude in the wilderness, soon followed him. He consequently became the founder of the first laura monastery in the Bethlehem Wilderness, known as Pharan after the nearby spring. He later established other lauras at the Mount of Temptation (see R11) and in Wadi Khureitun (see R34 and R35). The monastery was destroyed by Persians in 614 and rebuilt with assistance from the Czar of Russia in the 19th century.

Just beyond is the British Mandate pumping station with its eucalyptus trees. The first-century BC aqueduct of Herod also starts here, taking water to Ain Fawwar spring, thence to Ain Qelt spring, from where the combined waters went to Kypros and Herod's Temple at Tulul abu Alaeiq, near Jericho: an impressive project for 2000 years ago!

From Ain Fara, the wadi goes wild again almost until meeting the winding N–S road of 'Derekh Alon' or 'Way of Alon', an Israeli road originally meant to assist in securing their E border. During the 1967 war there were frequent clashes here with the Palestinian resistance.

The spring of Ain Fawwar, where this section of the trail ends a little further on, is not only welcome (there is a café) but also of interest. It is an 'on-off' (or intermittent) spring, alternately gushing and stopping at regular intervals due to the u-bend nature of the underground supply. You can take a refreshing dip in the spring and replenish your water from the source in the café – even free ice is available!

Flora and fauna See R23.

Special advice This trek includes the wildest parts of the whole Wadi Qelt. Precise route finding is not always fully obvious (despite trail marking). Be aware of flash flood risk.

Map SPNI 8

Map ref start (Hizma) 1755 1383;   Map ref start (alternative) 1755 1390   Map ref finish (Ain Fawwar) 1832 1387

Also refer to map with R23

Approach See R23.

The route From Hizma, walk E for 1km on a track which eventually descends L into Wadi Qelt, in which it arrives at an area of ancient terracing. (Alternatively, if you start from the bypass road, go past the prehistoric structures and descend into the wadi where the riverbed is formed of limestone pavement. Continue down, taking paths on the R bank at the point where the wadi bed drops. Follow these paths along,

Datura, Wadi Qelt

between cliffs, to descend through ancient terracing and meet the track from Hizma.)

Just beyond, Wadi Sunam enters from the R. The old Palestinian village trail crosses it and rises a little to contour along above the cliffs which fall vertically into the increasingly impressive limestone canyon. (Note the shepherds' caves in the opposite cliff.) Continue on the path, passing directly below the intrusively incongruous settlement of Almon, to reach an old stone wall. Beyond, the path zigzags steeply down to reach the ruins of the third-century Greek Orthodox monastery built by Chariton. The spring of Ain Fara is just beyond. This is about 5km (2hrs) from the start. (Climbers will have noted the quality of the limestone cliffs and will be interested to see the sign near the spring with the message 'Climbing and rappelling only on the north cliff'.)

Continuing down the valley, the trail passes by eucalyptus trees and the pumping station, from which a steel pipe heads off into the hills to the N before running parallel to the wadi. (It has blue trail markers and provides an alternative, but longer, 'high-level' route for those seeking to avoid the more adventurous route down the canyon.)

200m or so beyond the point where the pipe leaves the valley bottom, the trail we are taking climbs the R bank for a few metres, near a small cliff, to meet the ancient clay pipe aqueduct. Follow this along the cliff, then continue down the gorge taking the best choice of paths and frequently crossing the stream (sometimes tricky as mint and other vegetation conceal the water).

Eventually the path squeezes along the R bank between the cliffs and a jungle of bamboo-like fragmites, finishing by a Grade 2 traverse across the polished limestone cliff before descending to a 'beach'. Here, the path crosses the stream to the L side, then eventually back R and along limestone terraces above the 'jungle'-filled stream. It then descends into the fragmites thickets again and, squeezing along on the water's edge, emerges in a more open area with a rough open hillside on the R.

Follow the blue markers with some scrambling (Grade 1) to gain a track 50m or so above and R of the wadi, then follow the clay pipe along once more out into the bare, open desert hills. The steel pipe on the L bank descends from the hills just ahead, beyond which the wadi passes beneath the Derekh Alon Road. Now on a red-marked trail, follow the wadi down to emerge almost immediately at the spring of Ain Fawar (café, small natural pool and toilets). The friendly café also has a phone and information on the area.

If you are continuing down the wadi see R25, otherwise:

Return Pre-arrange a taxi, or it may be possible to ring from the café. Otherwise you would probably have to walk out up to the highway, which would be a bit grim! A road goes immediately to the Derekh Alon Road 458, which climbs steeply up S for 4km to meet Road 1 midway between Jericho and Jerusalem (about 15km either way). From there you can get a servis or bus.

Transport and accommodation See notes on Jericho preceding R12, and taxi information following R23.

Suitably refreshed, you can continue:

R25 Lower Wadi Qelt

'Through a tremendous gorge between the hills – one of the most picturesque ravines in Palestine – flows the Kelt. It is for a great part of the year a murmuring, silver stream, flowing between banks of oleander and strips of canes, through a narrow glen, which is just wide enough for it to pass. The ravine itself is 500 feet deep, and on its north bank a Greek monastery rests on the side of a precipice, which is almost perpendicular from top to bottom'

Palestine Past and Present, L. Valentine, circa 1919

The wild wadi eventually gives way to a most unusual trek alongside an aqueduct of rushing, gurgling water high in the barren hills. It emerges at the sensational St George's Monastery from which a good track descends through the rocky gorge to Jericho. Another great day out!

Moderate trek. 10km to St George's. 15km to Jericho. 5–6hrs, more to include the monastery. The route descends from 300m at Ain Fawwar to minus 100m at St George's, or minus 250m at Jericho.

Special interest The first point of interest is right at the start – the peculiar 'on-off' spring of Ain Fawwar, alternately gushing then ceasing (see R24). The ancient Hasmonean aqueduct, which was later repaired by Herod, starts here, heading down to Jericho. Sections of the old clay pipe will be seen along the way.

Lower down the wadi, the waterfall at Ain Qelt provides a refreshing and very welcome shower on a hot day. From there, a relatively modern aqueduct built on the line of a Second Temple aqueduct contours the dry hills all the way to St George's and on to Jericho. This 'new'

Fragmites reeds, Wadi Qelt

Mary Hartley

aqueduct was built in 1919 by the Palestinian Husseini family. There is a sign in neat Arabic script, dedicated to his memory:

'In the name of Allah, the Merciful, hundreds of years have passed since the wadi's water was lost until inspiration came from Allah to the working man and genius M'chaii ad Din Mustapha Hilili el Husseini in 1297 of the Hijra. He built the dam and the mill and restored the gardens in 1332 of the Hijra, and built the aqueduct that carries water to the fields of Aqabat Jabr that is south of the city of Jericho.'

Our route follows the aqueduct down as it passes over ancient bridges spanning dry wadis. Along the way, Ka'abneh Bedouin camps benefit from its water before it descends past the cliff-hanging fifth-century Monastery of St George of Koziba. See R12 (Nativity Trail).

Flora and fauna See R23.

Special advice As with the Upper Wadi Qelt, beware of flash floods at least as far as Ain Qelt. Route finding in the early stages is not always obvious, despite the trail marks. Take particular care to find the exit point just over 2km down from Ain Fawwar. Once you reach the aqueduct at Ain Qelt the going is much easier and quite unique, walking alongside a rippling stream in the midst of desert hills. (Don't be tempted to drink the water – as always, take plenty with you.) Have adequate clothes to dress decently if you intend entering St George's.

Map SPNI 8
Map ref start 1832 1387; Map ref finish (St George's) 1890 1390
Map ref finish (Jericho) 1935 1404   Also refer to map with R23

Approach Take a servis or bus along the Jerusalem–Jericho Road 1 for about 15km (half-way) to its junction with the Derekh Alon Road. Ain Fawwar is about 4km down this road (Road 458), turning R just before the bottom. The best way to access this point would really be by taxi.

The route From the spring and café go down the wadi, which narrows again into a canyon before 1km. Continue down, taking a rock terrace on the L side. Opposite, a cascade of water escaping from the aqueduct on the R side has turned the bare hillside green with vegetation.

Keep following the wadi down (red trail marks) with some scrambling, after which it widens out. Just beyond (about 3km from Ain Fawwar) there is a cliff on the R with a huge natural arch through it. The trail marks do not seem obvious here (at least we didn't see them at first!). If you look around, you should see one up on the hillside to the L. This is the way to go. (If you miss this, you will re-enter a canyon which becomes blocked with huge boulders, making the going difficult, and the red trail marks are absent – if you go that way in winter there are waterfalls and pools, making it necessary to swim – but beware of flooding! Going this way will also add to your time.)

Back on the red-marked trail, scramble up the L hillside for 50m or so to find a good path contouring the hill above the gorge. After about 1km, it reaches a rocky vantage point, then descends to a bridge and aqueduct emerging from the canyon. (It could be busy here at weekend.) Ain Qelt and its waterfall are 50m upstream – enjoy it!

From here, the next half of the trek is easy. Follow the aqueduct along the L side of the wadi, passing ancient arches to reach a sign pointing down past a Bedouin camp to St George's Monastery after about 1.5km. Leave the aqueduct here and go down into the valley to find more signs before reaching the bottom. Take the green trail signed St George's, which goes along the hillside – much more enjoyable and with better views than the red trail, which follows the dry river bed.

The green trail contours the L (N) hillside, eventually meeting the same aqueduct again before passing by a cluster of old houses, home to settled Bedouin. Continue along the aqueduct until it plunges down to join the other aqueduct by a bridge across the valley. Just beyond here a large cross marks a stunning view of St George's Monastery clinging to the cliff in a savage rock canyon. Take the zigzag path down to reach it.

From the monastery, either take the return route up to the highway or continue down the good track for a further 2km or so, passing by some hermitages, to reach the road leading into Jericho past Herod's Temple.

Return, accommodation, transport See R23 and notes on Jericho preceding R12.

There are two other popular, enjoyable and less demanding versions of the Wadi Qelt Trek, taking in the lower sections of the trail and visiting the famous monastery:

R26 Ain Qelt to St George's Monastery

'Who cuts a channel for the torrents of rain, and a path for the thunderstorm, to water a land where no man lives, a desert with no one in it, to satisfy a desolate wasteland and make it sprout with grass?'

Job 38: 25–27, *Holy Bible, NIV*

A pleasant and easy walk in wild hills alongside the cool, gurgling water of an aqueduct. A bizarre way to experience desert hills!

Easy walk. 6km. 3hrs. Allow more for a shower in the waterfall, a relaxing walk and a trip round the monastery. The route descends from 168m to St George's (which is 100m below sea level, though it's difficult to imagine).

Special interest, Flora and fauna See R12

Special advice Don't drink the water at Ain Qelt or in the aqueduct! Dress decently to enter the monastery.

Mary Hardey

Cotton thistle

Map SPNI 8

Map ref start 1869 1364;   Map ref finish (St George's) 1890 1390

Map ref finish (Jericho) 1935 1404

Also refer to map with R23

Approach Take a bus or servis from Jerusalem or Jericho along Road 1 to the sign marked Ein el Qelt.

The route Turn L (NE) off the main road at the sign for Ein Qelt, then L again immediately (by a petrol station). Follow the road down N to meet a larger road after about 0.5km. (This is the old 'Roman Road' to Jericho.) Here, go L then R to reach the dirt track going N to Wadi Qelt. There are some ruins here and a shaded viewpoint up on the small hill to the right (168m). Follow the rough road down to the wadi, passing above the ruins of the once very impressive bridge that supported the Herodian aqueduct to reach an old flourmill. Scramble up to the aqueduct on the N side of the wadi. Approximately ½–¾hr. (This approach has not been verified by the authors.)

Here, you could go L for a dip in the Ain Qelt waterfall before returning and following the lower part of R25 to St George's.

Return, accommodation, transport See R23 and notes on Jericho preceding R12.

The next route is a regular 'tourist trail':

R27 Jericho to St George's Monastery

Probably the most popular 'wilderness' walk in this guide, wild and rugged, but on a good track. Whichever way you go – up or down – it's an essential walk!

Easy walk. 5km. Allow 2hrs – more to include the monastery.

The route rises from minus 250m at Jericho to minus100m at St George's (even though you do feel up in the mountains!).

Special interest, Flora and fauna See R12 and R23.

Special advice Only a short walk, but wear sensible footwear; also, dress with respect for the monastery.

Map SPNI 8

Map ref start, Jericho 1935 1404;   Map ref finish, St George's 1890 1390 Also refer to map with R23

Approach Start from Jericho, or be lazy and take a servis out to the foot of Wadi Qelt to save 2km!

The route As for R12 to St George's and the Roman road.

Return, transport, accommodation See R23 and notes on Jericho preceding R12.

From the Jericho/Dead Sea area there are also other routes up into the hills of the Bethlehem Wilderness:

R28 Nebi Musa to Jerusalem

'Some wandered in desert wastelands, finding no way to a city where they could settle. They were hungry and thirsty, and their lives ebbed away. Then they cried out to the Lord in their trouble, and he delivered them from their distress.'

Psalm 107: 4–6, *Holy Bible, NIV*

The route passes by the historical desert sites of Hyrcania and Jebel Muntar, where the ruined monastery of St John is located. Jebel Muntar,

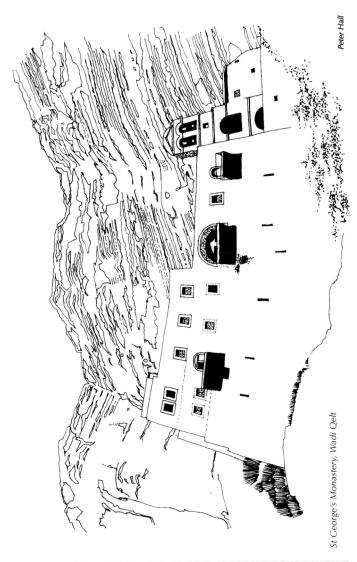

Peter Hall

St George's Monastery, Wadi Qelt

524m, is also the highest summit in this area and an excellent viewpoint. A useful route for those who take a taxi to, or can be dropped of at, the starting point and who wish to finish in Jerusalem without further undue transport complications! Only verified by the authors as far as Jebel Muntar, after which we returned to R29.

Moderate trek. 13km. Allow 5–6hrs, climbing from 60m to 524m at Jebel Muntar, then descending to approximately 440m and climbing again to 560m. About 600m of ascent and 100m of descent in total. It is possible to do this route in reverse (also easier, with much more downhill). In this case, you would need to make arrangements to be met on arrival at the road (otherwise it's a further hot 11.5km to Nebi Musa).

Special interest, biblical reference, Special advice, approach, etc See R13. On days other than Jewish weekends and holidays, remember to phone the IDF number for access.

Map SPNI 8

Map ref Nebi Musa 1910 1328;	Map ref start 1861 1238
Map ref Hyrcania 1848 1252;	Map ref Jebel Muntar 1828 1269
Map ref finish 1815 1235	Also refer to map with R30

The route Follow R13 to the 'crossroads' above Hyrcania (about 4km) then take the obvious 4wd track W to the face of the mountain directly ahead. Take the fork that goes diagonally L across the side of the hill instead of the steep 'full-frontal attack'! This brings you in just over 1km to a huge platform on the S side of the mountain. The highest point and its ruins are immediately behind. Excellent panoramic views including Wadi Qidron (location of Mar Saba), the hilltop suburbs of Bethlehem and Jerusalem, and the Dead Sea with the Mountains of Moab in Jordan on its E shore.

From here follow the 4wd track, which can be seen continuing generally WNW. The track ends at the Israeli settlement of Kedar. Walk to the main road.

Return Take a servis from the Road 38 Wadi el Nar road junction down to the Old City of Jerusalem or SW to Bethlehem. For a special taxi see taxi information following R23 for Jerusalem or R13 for Bethlehem.

For those wishing to return to the starting point on the Nebi Musa road, the following is a good alternative:

R29 Nebi Musa – Mar Saba round-trip

All the interest of R28 plus a magnificent view of Mar Saba, followed by a dusty downhill walk through barren desert used as an Israeli military training area and consequently littered with scrapped tanks and other unsightly junk.

Moderate trek. 14km. Allow 5hrs. Over 300m of ascent and descent.

Special interest, Special advice, map information, approach, etc As R13. On non-Jewish holidays, phone first for IDF clearance. Always leave visible information in your car, giving date, route taken and expected time of return.

Map SPNI 8

Map ref Nebi Musa 1910 1328; Map ref start and finish 1861 1238
Map ref Hyrcania 1848 1252;   Map ref Mar Saba view point 1817 1237 Also refer to map with R30

The route Follow R13 to the monastery viewpoint, but instead of continuing go back up the track to the main piste. Turn R and follow the 4wd track SE then E for just over 4km of dry, dusty walking to reach your starting point.

Return If you are not in your own transport it is essential that you pre-arrange to be met. For taxi contacts from Jericho, see information preceding R12.

A good way of reaching Mar Saba is to walk down from the hills of Bethlehem:

R30 Bethlehem to Mar Saba

'With joy you will draw water from the wells of salvation.'
                                        Isaiah 12: 3, *Holy Bible, NIV*

A delightful, predominantly downhill walk from the E suburbs of Bethlehem down rolling hills with ancient wells still used by Bedouin to the fifth-century Monastery of Mar Saba, which rises dramatically from the cliffs of Wadi Qidron. (R14, Day 10 of the Nativity Trail in reverse.) Excellent views along the way, especially E to the Dead Sea and the Mountains of Moab in Jordan.

Moderate trek. 8–9km. About 3hrs. Descending from about 600m to 250m with a gentle climb to 471m before descending again to about

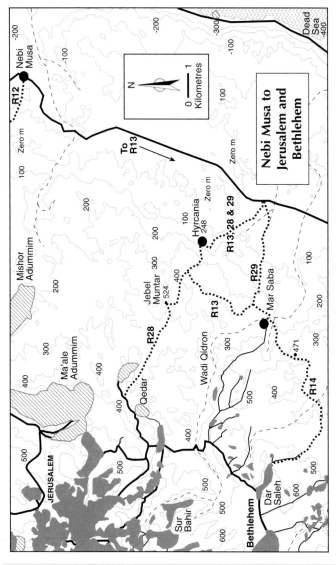

Nebi Musa to Jerusalem and Bethlehem

At the Wailing Wall, Jerusalem

On the Via Dolorosa, Jerusalem

250m at Mar Saba. About 570m of descent and 220m of ascent in total.

Special interest, Flora and fauna, Special advice See R14.

Map SPNI 8

Map ref start Dar Saleh 1767 1230;   Map ref Mar Saba 1815 1236

Approach From Bethlehem, take a servis up towards Dar Saleh. It will then be necessary to walk just over 0.5km up to an area of pine trees (named Ghalakto after a Greek Monk). Now, walk L to the mosque where a narrow road descends steeply R (SE). Alternatively take a special taxi to here (about 20NIS from Bethlehem).

The route Walk down the road following it R (small olive grove on L), then fork L between scattered houses with a small tell or hill beyond on the R. Follow the rough track down into the hills. A row of cave dwellings will be seen in the tell above the road (5mins from the start).

Continue down the track, which follows the crest of a rounded ridge to the junction of the two wadies (about 1.5km from start). Follow the merged wadies down for a further 1.5km, slowly swinging round towards the NE. About 3km (1hr) from the start take a side wadi, which enters from the left, and follow it up in a generally N direction to meet an old wall on its R (true L) flank. Follow the wall up and along, above the wadi, to reach a saddle about 4.5km from the start (about 1–1½hrs).

Careful observation will now reveal the stone cap of a well down to the NE, on a bare white hillside. You should also be able to see ancient water catchment channels leading into it, one actually crossing the saddle you are standing on.

Now in a more E direction, cross the wadi below and ascend the rocky ridge (past ancient stone threshing circles) to a shoulder with disused terraces on its R. Continue up, trending L to a saddle; then, still trending L, stroll up towards the crest of the ridge where there is an excavated grave. There are great panoramic views back to the edges of Bethlehem and Jerusalem and down to the Dead Sea and the Jordan Hills. One of the partially concealed Towers of Mar Saba can also be seen down to the NE. This point is 2hrs from the start (6km).

To reach Mar Saba, continue a little further up the rocky ridge, bearing L (NW) then N to reach the highest top (471m) with a deep valley on its R. Now, descend NE towards the Towers of Mar Saba, following a well-defined white ridge down. Contour round the L side of a final hump in the ridge and descend past a well to reach a dramatic wadi that drops steeply over water-polished rock to join the main

Qidron Gorge. Cross the smooth limestone bed of the wadi and follow a water catchment channel as it contours E above the main gorge to suddenly emerge at the monastery.

Return Unless you are continuing the walk down towards the Dead Sea or Nebi Musa (R13 in reverse) you will no doubt want to return to your base. In this case you should pre-arrange to be met at Mar Saba. See notes following R13 (for Bethlehem) or R23 (for Jerusalem).

Back in Bethlehem, it is worth spending some time exploring this ancient town:

BETHLEHEM

> *'But you, Bethlehem Ephrathah, though you are small among the clans of Judah, out of you will come for me one who will be ruler over Israel, whose origins are from of old, from ancient times.'*
>
> Micah 5: 2, *Holy Bible, NIV*

Bethlehem is pre-eminently Christ's birthplace, marked by the Church of Nativity in Manger Square. It also has much more to see, and the Bethlehem 2000 Project has done considerable work to identify walking circuits such as 'Harat Beit Lahem', 'The quarters of Bethlehem', which takes the visitor through ancient alleyways, under arches and past houses of architectural interest dating back to the 17th century. 'The Pilgrims' Route to the Shepherds' Field' goes from the historic core of Bethlehem along the historic way of the first pilgrims to the place where the star of Bethlehem was first seen. By walking and hiking in and around the town you will get to know the real Bethlehem and its people – an unforgettable experience.

For more information about places of interest and events in Bethlehem, see section in the Introduction 'Cultural heritage', also information following R14 or:

www.visit-palestine.com/bet/places/   www.bethlehem2000.org/beth-lehem

R31 Exploring Bethlehem

Hidden behind the bustling main streets of Bethlehem are a maze of interesting ancient alleyways and buildings. A system of walks designed by the Bethlehem 2000 Project takes you through them along Heritage and Discovery routes: a great way to see this town.

Easy walk. 5–8km, dependent on combination of routes taken. Allow 3hrs minimum, but much more to allow time in the holy places, museums etc. Perhaps 50–100m of descent and ascent.

Special interest Bethlehem has been inhabited for over 5000 years. It has been a pilgrimage destination since Christ was born where the Church of the Nativity now stands. The walks described will take you there via the Lutheran Christmas Church, the Old Market and other parts of the Old Bethlehem, with museums of Olive Pressing and Crafts. Beyond is the Milk Grotto. The route returns via the Peace Centre, the Mosque of Omar, the Nativity and Folklore museums, more crafts and old alleyways, the Syrian Orthodox church and, of course, numerous souvenir shops, cafés and restaurants.

Special advice Dress modestly with respect for the holy sites and local tradition. Check this and your other guidebooks for opening times of museums and churches. Look out for the Bethlehem 2000 Trail Signs.

Maps Bethlehem maps will be found in most Holy Land guidebooks. There is also an excellent 'Tourist Map of Bethlehem' from Geo Maps Centre, e-mail: geomsc@hotmail.com. The leaflet *Walking in the Old Town of Bethlehem* produced by Bethlehem 2000 applies specifically to the walks described here and is freely distributed, e-mail: info@bethlehem2000.org. The 'Map of Jerusalem and Bethlehem', Arab Hotel Association, is also useful. Tel: 02 6281805. Website: www.palestineho-tels.com

Approach From Jerusalem take a bus or servis from just W of the Damascus Gate (3NIS by servis). Either will probably terminate at the Bab al Z'qaq crossroads. Turn L here and

Peter Hall

Old olive press

163

Old Bethlehem doorway

Peter Hall

walk up the hill for about 0.5km to Madbasseh Square. The Lutheran Christmas Church is directly ahead.

The route From Madbasseh Square you have a choice of two routes, either side of the church. We took the street to the R. Just beyond an arch, take a side street L to explore the Old Market, with women in their embroidered dresses and a vast array of vegetable and fruit produce.

Returning R, back onto Najajereh Street again at the far end of the market, you emerge opposite the Olive Press Museum; a little further down, also on the R, are some narrow, stepped alleys and old houses renovated with help of the United Nations Development Programme. Plaques give details of donor countries. Exploring these, you will find a viewpoint S and SE to the distant hills of Hebron.

Up on Najajareh Street again, continue down to the bend, where more steps descend R to a lower street. Turn R for Al Ain Spring, which used to supply Bethlehem with water from the beautiful valley of Artas (R32). You are now about 1.25km from Madbasseh Square.

Return to the foot of the steps and walk along Anatreh Street for about 0.3km until some narrow alleys twist up L through ancient arches, bringing you to Milk Grotto Street. Turn R here and walk along, passing souvenir and craft shops, to the Milk Grotto Chapel, about 2.5km in total from Bab Z'qaq (2km from Madbasseh Square).

Return up Milk Grotto Street to arrive in Manger Square, location of the Church of Nativity. The Orient Palace Hotel and Peace Centre are opposite, and the Minaret of the Mosque of Omar marks a choice of exits from the square. Take either, passing souvenir shops and cafés, but continue up Paul V1 Street, which is R of the mosque to find the Old Bethlehem Home and Folklore Museum down an alley to the R, just beyond the mosque. This museum has been developed by local women to preserve the cultural heritage of Bethlehem. (You may, if you wish, continue down, past the museum between old houses to reach the new Mövenpick Hotel and the Crib Museum. Keep bearing R to re-emerge in Manger Square.)

Back on Paul VI Street, continue a short distance to the Peace Fountain before steps lead up to the Syrian Orthodox church (R) and alleys (L) into the Old Market visited earlier. (Or, go R then L to find a system of old alleys, archways and houses, which are worth exploring. This way emerges briefly onto Star Street before reascending via the Greek Orthodox church and Salesian Stairs to the Salesian church and Nativity Museum. Return L to re-enter Paul V1 Street after this 0.5km detour.) Here there are more souvenir and craft shops. Turn R along Paul V1 Street to come out at your starting point by the Christmas Church in Madbasseh Square.

Numerous other variations are possible on these Bethlehem 2000 walks which were created to help you explore Bethlehem and get to know its cultural heritage and people. Take your time and enjoy them.

Return To get back to Jerusalem, walk down to the Bab Z'qaq cross-roads and turn R. Wait just beyond the traffic lights for a servis. (Servis for Za'atara (near Herodion) (R34) start in the street below and L of Manger Square. Servis for Artas and Hebron start from the taxi park on the right of the road as you walk down from Madbasseh to Bab Z'qaq.)

And Artas is where we are going next, taking the road from Bethlehem towards Hebron, with a possible diversion to the old Palestinian village of:

EL KHADR

'Just before reaching Solomon's Pools, we came to an arch over a side-turning to the right. There was a plaque in the middle of the arch showing St George killing the dragon. After about a quarter of a mile till we came to the village called El-Khadr. ...El-Khadr means 'the green one', that is, the ever-young, undying one, a mythical prophet who, when on earth, drank from the waters of the Well of Life and became immortal. ...He is believed by Moslems and Christians of the Arab world to have been incarnated in the persons of both Elijah and St George. El-Khadr, as identified with Elijah, is also worshipped by the Eastern Jews, notably on Mount Carmel where there is a cave sacred to the prophet.

The Greek Orthodox Church in El-Khadr, which is otherwise a totally Moslem village, is dedicated to St George and attended by both Moslems and Christians. There are plenty of shrines to St George in the Arab world, but this church and the former cathedral at Lydda, now half-mosque and half-church, are the places where the saint is most revered in his home country, Palestine. ...When we left, I paused near the bell-tower to look across at the village. The flat roofs told one much about village life: on some, raisins and figs were drying in the sun, on one a sheep was tethered, on a few, washing was hanging out, on others bedding was spread out to air and some were piled high with brushwood. A wonderful peace and sense of timelessness pervaded the scene.'

St George – A Holy Land Saint, Delia Khano, 1985

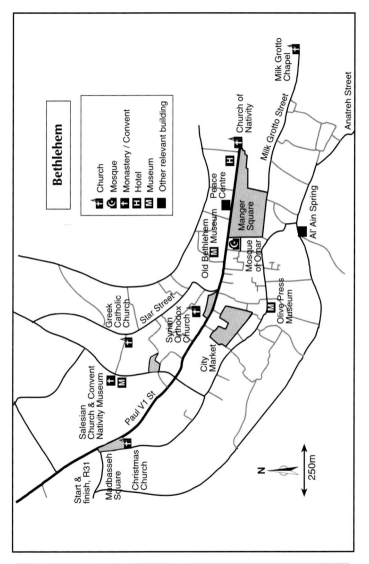

Bethlehem

Legend:
- ✝ Church
- ☾ Mosque
- ✝ Monastery / Convent
- H Hotel
- M Museum
- ■ Other relevant building

Milk Grotto Chapel
Anatreh Street
Milk Grotto Street
Church of Nativity
Peace Centre
Manger Square
Old Bethlehem Museum
Mosque of Omar
Al' Ain Spring
Olive Press Museum
Greek Catholic Church
Star Street
Syrian Orthodox Church
City Market
Salesian Church & Convent Nativity Museum
Paul VI St
Madbasseh Square
Christmas Church
Start & finish, R31

N
250m

Old Bethlehem street

Peter Hall

A little further towards Hebron, we arrive at the junction for Artas:

R32 Wadi Artas walk

'See how the lilies of the field grow. They do not labour or spin. Yet I tell you that not even Solomon in all his splendour was dressed like one of these.'

Mathew 6: 28–29, *Holy Bible, NIV*

Scenically beautiful, historically interesting and (if you take an Artas Museum Tour) a chance to learn about the area, its history, flora and fauna, and experience the local Palestinian food, culture and folklore heritage.

Easy walk. 3–4km, dependent on choice of route. Allow 2hrs. Descending from 810m to 750m, with a rise of 60m midway. Approximately 120m of descent and 60m of ascent in total. Not verified by the authors, who were only able to briefly visit Artas.

Special interest The beautiful valley of Artas has been inhabited by man since prehistoric times, due to the abundance of water from springs in the hills of Hebron. Two of them flow into the three 'Solomon's Pools' (which were not built by Solomon, but 800 years later in the Greek and Roman period to supply water to Jerusalem). The upper aqueduct, which is at 800m, dates from Herod's time and supplied water to Herodion (see R33 and R34). All were in use up to 1967. Other archaeological sites in this fertile valley include Byzantine and Crusader ruins and the remains of a 17th-century Ottoman fortress, Qalat el Burak.

Lower down the valley, in the village of Artas, a local resident, Musa Sanad, has created the Artas Folklore Museum and organises tours and folklore evenings to preserve the rich heritage of this Palestinian community. Opposite the village (the name of which derives from the Latin 'hortus' for 'garden', is the Convent of the Notre Dame de Hortus Conclusus built in 1902.

Flora and fauna The perennial springs and remarkable diversity of the terrain result in high biodiversity and richness of flora. Forests of pine cloak the sides of the narrow valley in which are vegetable gardens, olive groves and orchards of almonds and plums. Birdlife is plentiful.

Special advice You can, of course, walk in the Artas Valley without assistance, but the Artas Folklore Museum organises walks in the area with knowledgeable local Palestinian guides. Prices (including

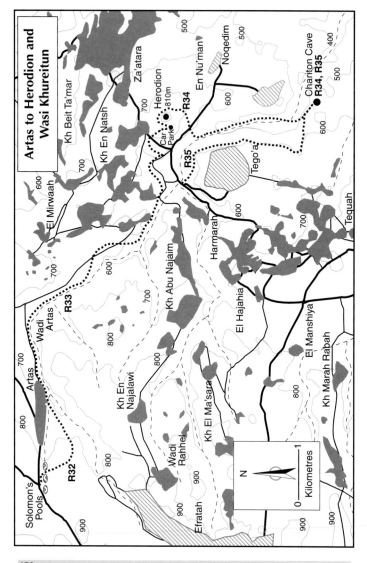

Artas to Herodion and Wasi Khureitun

excellent traditional food and folklore evenings) start from $36/head. Tel: Musa Sanad: 02 2744046. Groups of seven or more preferred. Alternatively, a visit to Artas Folklore Museum costs $3.

Map SPNI 8

Map ref Solomon's Pools (upper pool) 1660 1218 ;Map ref Artas village 1675 1218

Approach Artas is about 5km S of Bethlehem (1.5NIS by 'servis' taxi starting just up the road towards Manger Square from Bab Z'qaq). Ask for the Al Istiraha coffee shop, where the Artas road leaves the main Bethlehem–Hebron road. Qala'at el Burak is nearby, as are Ain Sahleh spring and Solomon's pools.

The route The route follows the L side of the pools then, S of the last one, goes up the hill passing water channels and the remains of water mills. The main channel that supplied the pools from the S (Birket Al Arroub) is at the top. It now goes SE in the valley, then passes near Ain Attan spring before ascending E to reach the top of the hill of Khirbet el Khoukh with good panoramic views. At this point the trail divides.

The longer way follows the slope S to see the ancient terraces of Wadi abu 'Amirah, still cultivated by the villagers. It then goes NE along the wadi before crossing the wadi to meet the short trail near the Roman pool and channel. Just beyond, it crosses again to avoid private property before reaching the wall of the Convent of Hortus Conclusus. Following it N, the trail meets the first village street, before continuing NE along the wall to the main road. (Here, it is worth a visit to the convent.) The trail then continues NE along the main road, and after two turns reaches the upper gate of Sitt Louise She'b (once the home of a Finnish lady who lived here in the early 20th century, writing about the life at that time). Down the steps and through the gate from its terraces, there is an excellent view of the convent and village houses rising from the valley, with the mosque's minaret piercing in the sky.

Continuing, a small path contours this high hill that dominates the valley, then goes into the valley along a dry-stone wall. To the left are the typical old houses of Artas village, originally built around natural or rock-cut caves. At the beginning of the valley, the trail crosses the second gate of Sitt Louise She'b, with Artas spring on its L.

Going S, the trail now enters Wadi Artas where, following the water channel, it reaches the Mameluke mill, which is worth exploring before continuing E past the so-called prisons, then N up steps to the Artas Village, location of the Folklore Centre and Museum.

The return From the Folk Museum, walk up the steep little hill to the upper village and catch a servis back to Bethlehem. Also see taxi information following R13.

This delightful walk can be extended all the way to Herod's unique hilltop citadel:

R33 Artas to Herodion (and back)

Follows the previous route to Artas village, then continues along the line of Herod's aqueduct to Herodion, with a possible return route if you're feeling fit.

Moderate trek. Approximately 12km. Allow 5hrs to enjoy the walk (or 8hrs for the round-trip, see 'Return' below). Starting from 810m, about 230m of descent and 60m of ascent in total, finishing on the road below Herodion. (And another 1km with 120m of ascent to reach its top, if you wish to continue.) Not verified by the authors.

Special interest, biblical references, Flora and fauna See R32.

Special advice Allow time to visit Artas Folklore Museum (see R32). The entry charge for Herodion is 15NIS.

Map SPNI 8

Map ref Solomon's Pools (upper pool) 1660 1218

Map ref Artas village 1675 1218; Map ref Herodion 1730 1193

Also refer to map with R32.

Approach As for R32.

The route Follow R32 to Artas village and Museum (3–4km). Here, go E through the village along the main street with traces of the Herodion channel to the L. To reach the peculiar volcano-shaped man-made hill of Herodion, which is visible ahead, follow tracks

Mary Hartley

Oleander

along the valley, which becomes less green as it approaches the dry desert hills.

Return It is possible to walk back, either by the same trail or by taking the road going S beneath Herodion crossing the wadi, then follow tracks E on the S side of the valley. The path reaches a cement channel that crosses Wadi Artas to the main road in front of the Artas Folklore Centre (approx. 8km, making 20km in total). Otherwise, take a taxi!

Taxis See R13 for Bethlehem, R23 for Jerusalem.

From Herodion, why not make a trek into Wadi Khureitun, the continuation of Wadi Artas, leading down into the Bethlehem Wilderness:

R34 Herodion to the Khureitun Cave

'The Fureidis was called Frank Mountain by the Crusaders, and must have been a strong fortification during all the ages in which isolated tells afforded the natural platform for castles. There is none of equal height and size in Palestine. Leaving it on the right, we had Bethlehem in full view about three miles westward, and the setting sun threw a mild and subdued light over the plains where the shepherds were keeping watch.'

The Land and the Book, W. M. Thomson, 1876

History and nature combine to give a nice round-trip in wild limestone scenery on the SE hills of Bethlehem, linking the impressive manmade hill of Herodion with the equally impressive natural cave system of Khureitun and the ruins of an old monastery. All sites are of historical importance.

Moderate trek. 9km for the round-trip. Allow at least 2hrs to reach the cave (and explore other points of interest along the way), and 1–1½hrs to return to the road. If you need to return all the way to Herodion add another 2km and 100m of ascent, making 11km in all. Allow another 1–2hrs if you intend exploring the passages shown here in Khureitun Cave (R35), making 5–6hrs in total. The walk involves over 200m of descent and 100m of ascent, some on scree or rocky terrain (some Grade 1 scrambling) starting from the Herodion car park at 730m. Some care necessary to find the path between cliffs.

Special interest The route starts from Herodion, the volcanic-shaped peak SE of Jerusalem and Bethlehem. The upper part of the hill was man-made by Herod the Great between 24 and 15BC to conceal his palace citadel. The view of the desert hills is excellent. Walking down the wadi, the route passes three caves in the L bank: the first is under a huge overhang, and still used by Bedouin. It has been in use since about 80,000BC. Next is a high triangular opening above the wadi – Um Qala, with signs of occupation from 8000BC. Continuing down, Um Qatafa was occupied as far back as the Lower Palaeolithic Period (90,000–1,500,000BC). The first signs of man's use of fire in Palestine were found here. At that time, the wadi would have had a river in it and the land was fertile with considerable wildlife. The Cave of Chariton – the object of the trek – was also used by man 500,000–1,000,000 years ago, and prehistoric remains include the oldest found in the Bethlehem wilderness.

In more recent times, around 340AD, it and about forty other 'laura cells' were used by monks and hermits, in particular the monk Chariton who used it as a retreat. He is considered to be the first of the monks to live in the wilderness and amongst the first leaders of the monastic movement in the Holy Land. The Monastery of Souka, or 'the Old Laura', the ruins of which are passed on the return journey, was built by Chariton in about 345AD and used until the 9th century. (Also see R24.) After Chariton, the best-known monk was Cyriac of Corinth (449–557AD). These days, the cave is also gaining fame as Palestine's most extensive cave system, with 3450m of passages!

Flora and fauna The upper valley of Khureitun is a nature reserve and International Birdlife Area. We saw a small herd of gazelles on the W side of the valley and found porcupine quills and evidence of this creature's digging activities.

Special advice Take care in route finding to pick the safest way and to find Khureitun Cave. If you are going to explore the cave (and others en route) you will need to carry torches and also extra gear (see R35). Beware of possible flash floods in the wadi bed.

Map SPNI 8

Map ref Herodion 1730 1193;   Map ref Khureitun Cave 1725 1168
Also refer to map with R32 and cave survey with R35

Approach From Bethlehem, you could take a servis from the bus station near Manger Square up to Za'atara, about 2km from Herodion, or towards Tequah, which is nearer. Otherwise, take a special taxi (see information following R13) to the entrance gate where there are toilets, cold water and a small shop. Entrance to Herodion is 15NIS.

The route From Herodion, the wadi or ravine of Khureitun is obvious to the SSW. It would be simple to head directly to it, but to add some interest why not include a circuit of Herod's Mountain? There are three tracks at the entry point. The upper one goes up to the top (15NIS). The central one goes part way round the hill (no need to pay). Follow it until it ends at a ramp of boulders and descend them to a lane.

Turn R onto the lane and follow it beneath the hill (olive grove on L) to a good view point to the E. Here, leave the lane and descend R down the slope, keeping well R of the new settlement (obvious by its water tower). Continue, crossing a track and passing beneath your starting point, having now walked round the hill, before descending R of olive groves to reach a road above the ravine.

Cross the road and descend R into a side valley in which a shepherds' track leads down past a well to the wadi bed. (Take care to follow the path as there are cliffs just above the valley floor.) Some old cave dwellings are obvious, on the other side. This point is about 2km from the start (less than 1hr).

From here, follow paths alongside the wadi bed (dry except after heavy rain), scrambling down the dry waterfall (Grade 1) before continuing along the wadi floor (more cave dwellings above, under overhangs on the L – see notes above) until a huge cave is seen, also on the L. Scramble 50m up to it to appreciate the spectacular rock scenery and explore the side passages and chambers (torch necessary). This point is about 2.5km from the start. (A cave survey in Hebrew is available from The Israeli Cave Research Centre – see 'Caving' in the Introduction.)

Mary Hartley

Cyclamen

Return to the wadi bed, descending another small, dry waterfall, and continue down the valley. Before reaching the bend below the settlement with its huge, obtrusive water tower high above to the L, scramble diagonally R up the hillside (some loose scree) to the foot of the cliffs visible ahead, high on the R skyline (4.5km from the start).

Follow paths beneath the cliffs, round the headland and across a little side valley. About 200m beyond, two prominent rectangular blocks on a ledge identify the entrance to Chariton's Cave. To reach them, continue along to reach a well-made path and a sign (in Hebrew). Scramble up from there on polished, slippery rock to a limestone ledge beneath overhangs. Walk along for 50m and climb blocks (Grade 1). The cave mouth is across a small gap (about 5km from the start). See R35 for more information on the cave.

The return leg of the trek is much more straightforward. Exit the cave, return N along the ledge and scramble down to the path with the sign. Follow the well-defined zigzag path up a side valley to reach the ruins of Souka at almost 0.5km from the cave. Here, leave the main path (which goes up to a settlement) and go R (N) again across the small valley to pass between more monastery ruins.

Just beyond the remains of a tower, the path splits. Take either and continue to contour N above Wadi Khureitun. The paths reunite after about 1km. A little over 1km further on, the path descends through a pretty area of pine forest with a Dolomitic ambience, eventually reaching the road at the head of the wadi, about 3.5km from the cave. If you need to return to Herodion car park, it's about 2km up the road to the NE.

Return Pre-arrange (or phone for) a special taxi back down to Bethlehem or Jerusalem. See information following R13 and R23.

Cavers who are specifically interested in exploring the cave could take a more direct approach:

R35 The Hanging Cave of Chariton

'Descending a savage ravine running down from the neighbourhood of Bethlehem for about five miles, and taking a very steep path or rather narrow ledge on which a fragment of rock bars the way, the entrance is reached. Only one person at a time can go through the narrow passage, which leads into a small cave. A winding gallery, thirty feet long, runs from it to the great cave. This is a hundred and twenty feet long and varies from thirty to forty five feet in breadth. It has a high arched roof of the natural rock.

The cave can only be seen by the light of candles or torches. In the dim light it is very impressive, and five narrow passages run from it in every direction, but all soon terminate in the rocky sides except one. Part of the way up this last passage is a pit, ten feet deep; beyond this is another long narrow passage which grows gradually lower and lower till those who pass through it have to crawl. Another large chamber seems to end the caves, but the Arabs say that they run underground to Tekoa.

A hundred yards above the cave, in a cleft in the rock, stand the ruins of a square tower, and foundations of some other part of the building – massive hewn stones. They are the remains of a monastery.'

Palestine Past and Present, L. Valentine, circa 1919

This is Palestine's largest cave system, with 3450m of passages! The cave, which is also of considerable historical significance, is situated in a superb position high on the W side of the beautiful limestone gorge of Wadi Khureitun, with excellent views.

Moderate cave. Experienced cavers only. Grade 2 if the passages on this cave map are followed. Over 250m in total, there and back. For the trip shown here, allow 1–2hrs, dependent on the size of the group, plus, of course, 2–3hrs to approach and return (about 3.5km each way). (Easy cave, Grade 1, if only the Cathedral Chamber is visited, or a serious cave if the full 3450m system is explored.)

Special interest See R34.

Special advice Unless you are experienced cavers, or with a guide who knows the cave, you should not go beyond the initial Cathedral Chamber: there is a warren of passages and you could easily get lost or have an accident. However, those with the necessary caving experience and equipment may wish to explore further. The initial 100m or so present some typical caving situations, narrow passages, a tight crawl, a rope descent (and ascent to get back) – perfect for a hot day!

For any part of the cave, good torches are essential. Head torches are best. At the time of our visit some passages were identified by string, and there was a frayed and slippery rope *in situ* to aid the polished 5m descent into the Deep Basin. If you intend to explore these passages beyond the first huge Cathedral Chamber you would be well advised to take 10m of good rope. Some of the passages and chambers have clay floors that no doubt become muddy after rain, due to seepage from above. Flooding seems unlikely, but the clay floor was damp when we were there, so take note of the weather forecast and be ready for the unexpected. Leave a note of your plans with a responsible person, including time of return, and notify them when you get back.

> **In conclusion, we will say again, if you are inexperienced do not wander far in the Cathedral Chamber unless you are sure of finding the way back, and definitely do not go beyond it.**

Map SPNI 8
Map ref Khureitun Cave 1725 1168
Also refer to map with R32

Experienced cavers wanting to explore the 3450m of the system should contact the Cave Research Centre for the cave survey – which is in Hebrew. (For contacts, see 'Caving' in the Introduction.)

Approach Either go via R34 or, if exploring the cave is your main interest, go directly to the cave by reversing the return leg of that route. Start from the big lay-by at the head of Wadi Khureitun, 2km SW of Herodion. Follow the track that descends into the wadi then leaves it to rise gently through the pine trees on its R bank. Following R34 in reverse, continue along the track, contouring S above Wadi Khureitun to reach the ruins of Souka Monastery after about 3km. Cross the little valley ahead and descend the good path to the foot of the cliff. Scramble up R to gain a limestone terrace and follow it 50m to reach the boulders marking the cave entrance.

The route Stride across the gap to enter the cave and take either passage in to reach the main Cathedral Chamber. The ongoing passage is over to the L. Follow it to a fork and go L through a tube where it is necessary to crawl to reach a small chamber. There, fork R and go through a passage with another chamber to reach a drop into The Basin. Descend into it with a rope for aid (possibly in situ) and cross it to the R. Climb out awkwardly to enter a passage at waist level. Follow this through two more chambers (past side and roof passage alternatives) to a big chamber beyond which are more passages. This was our furthest point. As people were waiting for us we returned to the entrance in case our absence was worrying them. Subsequent enquiries via the Cave Research Centre revealed that a complex system of passages lies ahead. Do not go beyond this point without the cave survey!

Return The reverse of the approach – as per R34. 1–1½ hours.

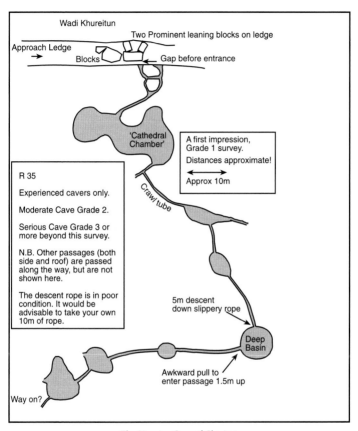

Wadi Khureitun

Two Prominent leaning blocks on ledge

Approach Ledge →

Blocks

Gap before entrance ←

'Cathedral Chamber'

A first impression, Grade 1 survey.

Distances approximate!

←→ Approx 10m

Crawl tube

R 35

Experienced cavers only.

Moderate Cave Grade 2.

Serious Cave Grade 3 or more beyond this survey.

N.B. Other passages (both side and roof) are passed along the way, but are not shown here.

The descent rope is in poor condition. It would be advisable to take your own 10m of rope.

5m descent down slippery rope

Deep Basin

Awkward pull to enter passage 1.5m up

Way on?

The Hanging Cave of Chariton

That's it for now folks – hope you enjoyed it all as much as we did!

APPENDICES

GRADED LIST OF ROUTES

The following list will give the reader an opportunity to see at a glance the number of routes in each grade, the length of the route and the time required.

Easy Walk		Distance (km)	Time
R2	Ascent of Mount Tabor	1.5	1hr
R9	Yanun to Duma	12	5hrs
R11	Auja to Jericho	13	5hrs
R15	Mount Tabor Circuit	2	1hr
R16	Exploring Nablus	2–3	half a day
R17	Wadi Zerqa and Wadi Natuf	12	5hrs
R18	The Shuqba Cave	1	1hr
R19	The Abud Cave	0.5	1hr
R20	Jerusalem Ramparts and Old City	6	4hrs–1 day
R21	The Palm Sunday Walk	4	3hrs or more
R22	Exploring Lifta	1	1hr or more
R26	Ain Qelt to St George's Monastery	6	3hrs or more
R27	Jericho to St George's Monastery	5	2hrs or more
R31	Exploring Bethlehem	5–8	3hrs or more
R32	Wadi Artas Walk	3–4	2hrs

Moderate Trek			
R3	Jezreel to Faqu'a	8–9	4–5hrs
R4	Nazareth to Mount Tabor	16	6hrs
R5	Mount Tabor to Faqu'a	43	2 days
R6	Faqu'a to Zababdeh	20	8–9hrs
R7	Zababdeh to Agrabanieh	21	8–9hrs
R8	Agrabanieh to Yanun	15	6–7hrs
R12	Jericho to Nebi Musa	14	5–6hrs
R13	Nebi Musa to Mar Saba	8	4hrs
R14	Mar Saba to Bethlehem	8–9	3–4hrs
R25	Lower Wadi Qelt to St George's	10	5–6hrs
R25	Lower Wadi Qelt to Jericho	15	8hrs
R28	Nebi Musa to Jerusalem	13	5–6hrs

R29	Nebi Musa-Mar Saba round-trip	14	5hrs
R30	Bethlehem to Mar Saba	8	3hrs
R33	Artas to Herodion	12	5hrs
R33	Artas to Herodion and back	20	8hrs
R34	Herodion to the Cave of Chariton	11	5–6hrs

Serious Trek		**Distance (km)**	**Time**
R1	Nativity Trail	150	10 days
R10	Duma to Ain Auja	18	7–8hrs
R23	Wadi Qelt	25	1 day
R24	Upper Wadi Qelt	10	4–6hrs

Easy Cave

R18 The Shuqba Cave

R19 The Abud Cave

R35 The Hanging Cave of Chariton to the Cathedral Chamber

Moderate Cave

R35 The Hanging Cave of Chariton initial passages

Serious Cave

R35 The Hanging Cave of Chariton – full 3450m system

SOME USEFUL ARABIC/ENGLISH WORDS

Topographical words

ain (ein)	spring (of water)
bilad	village, town
bir	well, cistern (of water)
birkat	pool
bustan	garden (usually of vegetables)
ghor	low lying desert
hammamat	hot spring
jebel (jabal)	mountain
khirbet	ruins
maghrar (magharah)	cave
maqam	Muslim shrine (tomb)
mazraa	fields (agricultural area/farm)
qasr	castle
qattar	dripping spring
rijm	cairn, tower
sahil	plain, plateau
siq	rock crevasse, narrow canyon
tell	prehistoric hill, mound
wadi	seasonal river, desert valley

A few other useful words

bread	khubis
coffee	kahwah
tea	shai
water	maya (maa)
shop	dukkan
here	huna
there	hunak
where?	wayn?
left	yssar (shimal)
right	yemeen
straight on	dughri
north	shamal

south	jannub
east	sharq
west	gharb
road	tareeq
path	tareeq turabi
where is the path to ...?	min wayn el tareeq ila ...?
thanks	shokran
hello	marhaba
how are you?	kayf halak (m) kayf halik (f)
very well (thanks be to God)	quais (el hamdulillah) (m)
very well (thanks be to God)	quaisa (el hamdulillah) (f)

GLOSSARY

bivouac	sleep out without tent
cairn	a pile of stones to mark the way
col	a low region of land between two hills
crag	cliff
dale	valley
escarpment	long cliff
gully	a narrow ravine
pass	see 'col'
karst	limestone affected by water dissolution
laura	a collecton of monk's cells or hermitages
saddle	see 'col'
scree	a slope of loose stones
slab	less than vertical rock
tell	prehistoric hill, mound
wadi	a desert valley or seasonal riverbed

USEFUL BOOKS AND WEBSITES

First, we should mention the Holy Bible, New International Version – even if you are an atheist you may find it interesting to refer to both Old and New Testaments. Next, something rather more up to date and available free in hotels, etc: *This Week in Palestine*, a kind of *What's On* that comes out monthly despite its name! Finally, here's some relevant reading in dated order. (Some of the older books may be difficult to get unless they have been republished.)

BACKGROUND READING

The Land and the Book, W. M. Thomson. T. Nelson and Sons, London, 1876

The Historical Geography of the Holy Land, George Adam Smith, 1894, 30th edition, 4th impression. HarperCollins Publishers Ltd, 1974

Palestine Past and Present, L. Valentine. Frederick Warne and Co., c.1919

In the Steps of the Master, H. V. Morton. Rich and Cowan, 1934. Future editions from Methuen.

Blood Brothers, Father Elias Chacour. Kingsway Publishers, 1984

Arab and Jew. Wounded Spirits in a Promised Land, David K. Shipler. Times Books, 1986

Palestinian Costume, Shelagh Weir. British Museum Press, 1989

The Palestinian Village Home, Suad Amiry and Vera Tamari. British Museum Publication, 1989

We Belong to the Land, Father Elias Chacour. Harper, San Francisco, 1990

A History of Jerusalem, One City, Three Faiths, Karen Armstrong. Harper Collins, 1996

Twenty Centuries of Christian Pilgrimage to the Holy Land, Nathan Schur. Dvir Publishing, 1992

The Question of Palestine, Edward W. Said. Vintage, 1992

Before the Mountains Disappear, Ali H. Qleibo. Kloreus Books, 1992

I am a Palestinian Christian, Mitri Raheb. Augsburg Fortress Press, 1995

The Invention of Ancient Israel: The Silencing of Palestinian History, Prof Wilhelm. Routledge, 1996

Bethlehem 2000, Mitri Raheb and Fred Strickert. Palmyra, 1998

From the Holy Mountain, William Dalrymple. Flamingo, 1998

Domestic Life in Palestine, Mary Eliza Rogers. KPI Paperbacks

Living Stones Pilgrimage, Alison Hilliard & Betty Baily, Cassell 1999

Jerusalem in the Heart, Ali H Qleibo. Kloreus Books, 2000

By Eastern Windows, Delia Khano. Guiding Star, 2000

Peace and its Discontents: Essays on Palestine in the Middle East Process, Edward W. Said.

Before their Diaspara: A Photographic History of the Palestinians, Walid Khalildi

Travel Guides

Guide to the Holy Land, Eugene Hoad. Franciscan Printing Press, Jerusalem, 1984

The Holy Land. The Indispensable Archaeological Guide for Travellers, Jerome Murphy-O'Connor. Oxford University Press 3rd edition 1992

Landscapes of the Holy Land, Susan Arenz. Sunflower Books, 1997

Israel and Palestinian Territories. Rough Guide, 1998

Beyond the Walls – Churches of Jerusalem, Aviva Bar-am. 1998

Every Pilgrim's Guide to the Holy Land, N. Wareham and J. Gill. Canterbury Press, 1998

Israel Handbook with the Palestinian Authority Areas, Dave Winter and John Matthews. Footprint Handbooks, Passport Books, 1998

Mini Rough Guide to Jerusalem, Daniel Jacobs. Rough Guides Ltd, 1999

Israel and Palestinian Territories. Lonely Planet, 1999

Palestine. West Bank and Gaza Strip, Dr Adel Yahya. PACE Tour Guide, 1999

Jerusalem – the Holy Land. Dorling Kindersley Travel Guides, 2000

Palestine with Jerusalem, H. Stedman. Bradt Travel Guides, 2000

A Third Millennium Guide to Pilgrimage to the Holy Land, ed. Duncan MacPherson. Melisende Publishing, 2000

Jouney into the Holy Land, (meditations and reflections written on the Nativity Trail), Susan Sayers, Kevin Mayhew Ltd, 2001

Flora and Fauna

The Birds of the Hashemite Kingdom of Jordan, Ian J. Andrews. 1995

Mammals of the Holy Land, Mazin B. Qumsiyeh. Texas Tech University Press, 1996

Wild Flowers of Jordan and Neighbouring Countries, Dawud M. H. Al-Eisawi. Jordan Press Foundation, Al Rai, 1998

Important Bird Areas in Palestine, Imad Atrash. Palestinian Wild Life Society (PWLS), 1999

Middle East Walks, Treks, Caves, Climbs and Canyons

'The Hanging Cave of Chariton', *Niqrot Zurim* [Journal of Israeli Cave Research Centre (ICRC)], 13 Oct 1986 (In Hebrew, some surveys of this and other caves)

Treks and Climbs in Wadi Rum, Jordan, Tony Howard. Cicerone Press, 1987; 3rd edn, 1997

Walks and Scrambles in Wadi Rum, Tony Howard and Di Taylor. Al Kutba, 1989. 4th edn, Jordan Distribution Agency, 2002. UK distributor, Cordee

An Introduction to the Caves of Oman, Samir Hanna and Mohammed el-Belushi. Motivate Publishing, 1996

Jerusalem – Easy Walks, Aviva Bar-am. 1999

Jordan – Walks, Treks, Caves, Climbs and Canyons, Di Taylor and Tony Howard. Cicerone Press, 1999

Trekking and Canyoning in the Jordanian Dead Sea Rift, Itai Haviv. Desert Breeze Press, 2000

Around the Holy City, Ammon Rammon. Jerusalem Institute for Israel Studies, 2000

Websites
Applied Research Institute in Jerusalem: www.arij.org
For information on maps, settlements, bypass roads, etc, add: /eyeinpalestine

Arabian information: www.arabia.com

Alternative Information Centre: www.aic.org

Alternative Tourism Group. For information on Nativity Trail etc: www.patg.com

Bethlehem 2000 Project: www.bethlehem2000.org/
Click tourism for Nativity Trail

Birzeit University (Palestine and the Nativity Trail): www.birzeit.edu/

British Consulate, Jerusalem: www.britishconsulate.org

Dheisheh Refugee Camp: www.dheisheh.acrossborders.org

Catholic Relief Services: www.catholicrelief.org/where/jerusalem/index.cfm

Christian Peacemakers Team: www.prairienet.org/cpt

Guiding Star. For Nativity Trail and other tours: www.guidingstarltd.com

Hotels of Palestine: www.palestinehotels.com

International Centre of Bethlehem: www.annadwa.org

Islamic Association for Palestine: www.iap.org

Israeli Information Centre for Human Rights (for the mass destruction of Palestinian houses on the West Bank, etc): www.btselem.org

Jerusalem Media and Communication Centre: www.jmcc.org

Khalil Sakakini Cultural Centre, Ramallah: www.sakakini.org

O.S Hotel Services, Jerusalem: www.oshotels.com

PACE (Palestinian Association for Cultural Exchange): www.planet.edu/~pace/

Palestine Report: www.jmcc.org/media/reportonline

Palestinian Centre for Rapprochement between People: www.rapprochement.org

Palestinian Ministry of Environmental Affairs (MEnA): www.menah@palnet.com

Palestinian Ministry of Tourism and Antiquities: www.visit-palestine.com

Palestinian National Authority: www.pna.org www.pna.org

Palestinian Wildlife Society (PWLS): www.wildlife-pal.org

Popular Arts Centre: www.popularartcentre.org

Sabeel Ecumenical Liberation Theology Centre: www.sabeel.org

Welcome to Palestine – land, people and culture: www.palestine-net.co

Dedication

إهداء

أعدّت هيئة مشروع بيت لحم ٢٠٠٠ هذا الكتاب إسهاماً منها في دعم التنمية الاقتصادية في فلسطين و هي تهديه لجميع الفلسطينيين الذين كانت لديهم الرؤية فآمنوا بالمشروع و عملوا على تحقيق أهدافه ودعموه في الأوقات الصعبة، كما تهديه لهؤلاء الذين قابلناهم في تجوالنا، في الهضاب و الوديان، في القرى والبلدات، و الذين مدوا لنا يد العون وتمنوا لنا النجاح في مسعانا، و إننا على ثقة أن هذا الكتاب سيسهم فعلاً في تعريف الزوار القادمين إلى الأراضي المقدسة بفلسطين و شعبها.

هيئة مشروع بيت لحم ٢٠٠٠

٢٩ تشرين ثاني ٢٠٠٠

LISTING OF CICERONE GUIDES

NORTHERN ENGLAND

LONG DISTANCE TRAILS

THE DALES WAY
THE ISLE OF MAN COASTAL PATH
THE PENNINE WAY
THE ALTERNATIVE COAST TO COAST
NORTHERN COAST-TO-COAST WALK
THE RELATIVE HILLS OF BRITAIN
MOUNTAINS ENGLAND & WALES
VOL 1 WALES. VOL 2 ENGLAND.

CYCLING

BORDER COUNTRY BIKE ROUTES
THE CHESHIRE CYCLE WAY
THE CUMBRIA CYCLE WAY
THE DANUBE CYCLE WAY
LANDS END TO JOHN O'GROATS
CYCLE GUIDE
ON THE RUFFSTUFF -
84 Bike Rides in Nth Engl'd
RURAL RIDES No.1 WEST SURREY
RURAL RIDES No.1 EAST SURREY
SOUTH LAKELAND CYCLE RIDES
THE WAY OF ST JAMES
Le Puy to Santiago - Cyclist's

LAKE DISTRICT AND MORCOMBE BAY

CONISTON COPPER MINES
CUMBRIA WAY & ALLERDALE RAMBLE
THE CHRONICLES OF MILNTHORPE
THE EDEN WAY
FROM FELL AND FIELD
KENDAL - A SOCIAL HISTORY
A LAKE DISTRICT ANGLER''S GUIDE
LAKELAND TOWNS
LAKELAND VILLAGES
LAKELAND PANORAMAS
THE LOST RESORT?
SCRAMBLES IN THE LAKE DISTRICT
MORE SCRAMBLES IN THE
LAKE DISTRICT
SHORT WALKS IN LAKELAND
Book 1: SOUTH
Book 2: NORTH
Book 3: WEST
ROCKY RAMBLER'S WILD WALKS
RAIN OR SHINE
ROADS AND TRACKS OF THE
LAKE DISTRICT
THE TARNS OF LAKELAND Vol 1: West
THE TARNS OF LAKELAND Vol 2: East
WALKING ROUND THE LAKES
WALKS SILVERDALE/ARNSIDE
WINTER CLIMBS IN LAKE DISTRICT

NORTH-WEST ENGLAND

WALKING IN CHESHIRE
FAMILY WALKS IN FOREST OF
BOWLAND
WALKING IN THE FOREST OF
BOWLAND
LANCASTER CANAL WALKS

WALKER'S GUIDE TO LANCASTER
CANAL
CANAL WALKS VOL 1: NORTH
WALKS FROM THE LEEDS-LIVERPOOL
CANAL
THE RIBBLE WAY
WALKS IN RIBBLE COUNTRY
WALKING IN LANCASHIRE
WALKS ON THE WEST PENNINE
MOORS
WALKS IN LANCASHIRE WITCH
COUNTRY
HADRIAN'S WALL
Vol 1 : The Wall Walk
Vol 2 : Wall Country Walks

NORTH-EAST ENGLAND

NORTH YORKS MOORS
THE REIVER'S WAY
THE TEESDALE WAY
WALKING IN COUNTY DURHAM
WALKING IN THE NORTH PENNINES
WALKING IN NORTHUMBERLAND
WALKING IN THE WOLDS
WALKS IN THE NORTH YORK MOORS
Books 1 and 2
WALKS IN THE YORKSHIRE DALES
Books 1,2 and 3
WALKS IN DALES COUNTRY
WATERFALL WALKS - TEESDALE &
HIGH PENNINES
THE YORKSHIRE DALES
YORKSHIRE DALES ANGLER'S GUIDE

THE PEAK DISTRICT

STAR FAMILY WALKS PEAK
DISTRICT/Sth YORKS
HIGH PEAK WALKS
WEEKEND WALKS IN THE PEAK
DISTRICT
WHITE PEAK WALKS
Vol.1 Northern Dales
Vol.2 Southern Dales
WHITE PEAK WAY
WALKING IN PEAKLAND
WALKING IN SHERWOOD FORES
WALKING IN STAFFORDSHIRE
THE VIKING WAY

WALES AND WELSH BORDERS

ANGLESEY COAST WALKS
ASCENT OF SNOWDON
THE BRECON BEACONS
CLWYD ROCK
HEREFORD & THE WYE VALLEY
HILLWALKING IN SNOWDONIA
HILLWALKING IN WALES Vol.1
HILLWALKING IN WALES Vol.2
LLEYN PENINSULA COASTAL PATH
WALKING OFFA'S DYKE PATH
THE PEMBROKESHIRE COASTAL PATH
THE RIDGES OF SNOWDONIA
SARN HELEN
SCRAMBLES IN SNOWDONIA
SEVERN WALKS

THE SHROPSHIRE HILLS
THE SHROPSHIRE WAY
SPIRIT PATHS OF WALES
WALKING DOWN THE WYE
A WELSH COAST TO COAST WALK
WELSH WINTER CLIMBS

THE MIDLANDS

CANAL WALKS VOL 2: MIDLANDS
THE COTSWOLD WAY
COTSWOLD WALKS Book 1: North
COTSWOLD WALKS Book 2: Central
COTSWOLD WALKS Book 3: South
THE GRAND UNION CANAL WALK
HEART OF ENGLAND WALKS
WALKING IN OXFORDSHIRE
WALKING IN WARWICKSHIRE
WALKING IN WORCESTERSHIRE
WEST MIDLANDS ROCK

SOUTH AND SOUTH-WEST ENGLAND

WALKING IN BEDFORDSHIRE
WALKING IN BUCKINGHAMSHIRE
CHANNEL ISLAND WALKS
CORNISH ROCK
WALKING IN CORNWALL
WALKING IN THE CHILTERNS
WALKING ON DARTMOOR
WALKING IN DEVON
WALKING IN DORSET
CANAL WALKS VOL 3: SOUTH
EXMOOR & THE QUANTOCKS
THE GREATER RIDGEWAY
WALKING IN HAMPSHIRE
THE ISLE OF WIGHT
THE KENNET & AVON WALK
THE LEA VALLEY WALK
LONDON THEME WALKS
THE NORTH DOWNS WAY
THE SOUTH DOWNS WAY
THE ISLES OF SCILLY
THE SOUTHERN COAST TO COAST
SOUTH WEST WAY
Vol.1 Mineh'd to Penz.
Vol.2 Penz. to Poole
WALKING IN SOMERSET
WALKING IN SUSSEX
THE THAMES PATH
TWO MOORS WAY
WALKS IN KENT Book 1
WALKS IN KENT Book 2
THE WEALDWAY & VANGUARD WAY

SCOTLAND

WALKING IN THE ISLE OF ARRAN
THE BORDER COUNTRY -
A WALKERS GUIDE
BORDER COUNTRY CYCLE ROUTES
BORDER PUBS & INNS -
A WALKERS' GUIDE
CAIRNGORMS, Winter Climbs
5th Edition

LISTING OF CICERONE GUIDES

CENTRAL HIGHLANDS
  6 LONG DISTANCE WALKS
WALKING THE GALLOWAY HILLS
WALKING IN THE HEBRIDES
NORTH TO THE CAPE
THE ISLAND OF RHUM
THE ISLE OF SKYE A Walker's Guide
WALKS IN THE LAMMERMUIRS
WALKING IN THE LOWTHER HILLS
THE SCOTTISH GLENS SERIES
    1 - CAIRNGORM GLENS
    2 - ATHOLL GLENS
    3 - GLENS OF RANNOCH
    4 - GLENS OF TROSSACH
    5 - GLENS OF ARGYLL
    6 - THE GREAT GLEN
    7 - THE ANGUS GLENS
    8 - KNOYDART TO MORVERN
    9 - THE GLENS OF ROSS-SHIRE
SCOTTISH RAILWAY WALKS
SCRAMBLES IN LOCHABER
SCRAMBLES IN SKYE
SKI TOURING IN SCOTLAND
THE SPEYSIDE WAY
TORRIDON - A Walker's Guide
WALKS FROM THE WEST HIGHLAND
  RAILWAY
THE WEST HIGHLAND WAY
WINTER CLIMBS NEVIS & GLENCOE

IRELAND

IRISH COASTAL WALKS
THE IRISH COAST TO COAST
THE MOUNTAINS OF IRELAND

WALKING AND TREKKING IN THE ALPS

WALKING IN THE ALPS
100 HUT WALKS IN THE ALPS
CHAMONIX to ZERMATT
GRAND TOUR OF MONTE ROSA
  Vol. 1 and Vol. 2
TOUR OF MONT BLANC

FRANCE, BELGIUM AND LUXEMBOURG

WALKING IN THE ARDENNES
ROCK CLIMBS BELGIUM & LUX.
THE BRITTANY COASTAL PATH
CHAMONIX - MONT BLANC
  Walking Guide
WALKING IN THE CEVENNES
CORSICAN HIGH LEVEL ROUTE: GR20
THE ECRINS NATIONAL PARK
WALKING THE FRENCH ALPS: GR5
WALKING THE FRENCH GORGES
FRENCH ROCK
WALKING IN THE HAUTE SAVOIE
WALKING IN THE LANGUEDOC
TOUR OF THE OISANS: GR54
WALKING IN PROVENCE
THE PYRENEAN TRAIL: GR10
THE TOUR OF THE QUEYRAS

ROBERT LOUIS STEVENSON TRAIL
WALKING IN TARENTAISE &
  BEAUFORTAIN ALPS
ROCK CLIMBS IN THE VERDON
TOUR OF THE VANOISE
WALKS IN VOLCANO COUNTRY

FRANCE/SPAIN

ROCK CLIMBS IN THE PYRENEES
WALKS & CLIMBS IN THE PYRENEES
THE WAY OF ST JAMES
  Le Puy to Santiago - Walker's
THE WAY OF ST JAMES
  Le Puy to Santiago - Cyclist's

SPAIN AND PORTUGAL

WALKING IN THE ALGARVE
ANDALUSIAN ROCK CLIMBS
BIRDWATCHING IN MALLORCA
COSTA BLANCA ROCK
COSTA BLANCA WALKS VOL 1
COSTA BLANCA WALKS VOL 2
WALKING IN MALLORCA
ROCK CLIMBS IN MAJORCA, IBIZA &
  TENERIFE
WALKING IN MADEIRA
THE MOUNTAINS OF CENTRAL SPAIN
THE SPANISH PYRENEES GR11 2nd Ed.
WALKING IN THE SIERRA NEVADA
WALKS & CLIMBS IN THE PICOS DE
  EUROPA
VIA DE LA PLATA

SWITZERLAND

ALPINE PASS ROUTE, SWITZERLAND
THE BERNESE ALPS A Walking Guide
CENTRAL SWITZERLAND
THE JURA: HIGH ROUTE & SKI
  TRAVERSES
WALKING IN TICINO, SWITZERLAND
THE VALAIS, SWITZERLAND.
  A Walking Guide

GERMANY, AUSTRIA AND EASTERN EUROPE

MOUNTAIN WALKING IN AUSTRIA
WALKING IN THE BAVARIAN ALPS
WALKING IN THE BLACK FOREST
THE DANUBE CYCLE WAY
GERMANY'S ROMANTIC ROAD
WALKING IN THE HARZ MOUNTAINS
KING LUDWIG WAY
KLETTERSTEIG Northern Limestone Alps
WALKING THE RIVER RHINE TRAIL
THE MOUNTAINS OF ROMANIA
WALKING IN THE SALZKAMMERGUT
HUT-TO-HUT IN THE STUBAI ALPS
THE HIGH TATRAS

SCANDANAVIA

WALKING IN NORWAY
ST OLAV'S WAY

ITALY AND SLOVENIA

ALTA VIA - HIGH LEVEL WALKS
  DOLOMITES

CENTRAL APENNINES OF ITALY
WALKING CENTRAL ITALIAN ALPS
WALKING IN THE DOLOMITES
SHORTER WALKS IN THE DOLOMITES
WALKING ITALY'S GRAN PARADISO
LONG DISTANCE WALKS IN ITALY'S
  GRAN PARADISO
ITALIAN ROCK
WALKS IN THE JULIAN ALPS
WALKING IN SICILY
WALKING IN TUSCANY
VIA FERRATA SCRAMBLES IN THE
  DOLOMITES

OTHER MEDITERRANEAN COUNTRIES

THE ATLAS MOUNTAINS
WALKING IN CYPRUS
CRETE - THE WHITE MOUNTAINS
THE MOUNTAINS OF GREECE
JORDAN - Walks, Treks, Caves etc.
THE MOUNTAINS OF TURKEY
TREKS & CLIMBS WADI RUM JORDAN
CLIMBS & TREKS IN THE ALA DAG
WALKING IN PALESTINE

HIMALAYA

ADVENTURE TREKS IN NEPAL
ANNAPURNA - A TREKKER'S GUIDE
EVEREST - A TREKKERS' GUIDE
GARHWAL & KUMAON - A Trekker's
  Guide
KANGCHENJUNGA - A Trekker's Guide
LANGTANG, GOSAINKUND &
  HELAMBU Trekkers Guide
MANASLU - A trekker's guide

OTHER COUNTRIES

MOUNTAIN WALKING IN AFRICA -
  KENYA
OZ ROCK – AUSTRALIAN CRAGS
WALKING IN BRITISH COLUMBIA
TREKKING IN THE CAUCAUSUS
GRAND CANYON & AMERICAN
  SOUTH WEST
ROCK CLIMBS IN HONG KONG
ADVENTURE TREKS WEST NORTH
  AMERICA
CLASSIC TRAMPS IN NEW ZEALAND

TECHNIQUES AND EDUCATION

SNOW & ICE TECHNIQUES
ROPE TECHNIQUES
THE BOOK OF THE BIVVY
THE HILLWALKER'S MANUAL
THE TREKKER'S HANDBOOK
THE ADVENTURE ALTERNATIVE
BEYOND ADVENTURE
FAR HORIZONS - ADVENTURE
  TRAVEL FOR ALL
MOUNTAIN WEATHER

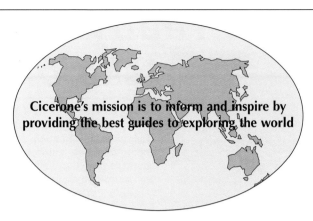

Cicerone's mission is to inform and inspire by providing the best guides to exploring the world

Since its foundation over 30 years ago, Cicerone has specialised in publishing guidebooks and has built a reputation for quality and reliability. It now publishes nearly 300 guides to the major destinations for outdoor enthusiasts, including Europe, UK and the rest of the world.

Written by leading and committed specialists, Cicerone guides are recognised as the most authoritative. They are full of information, maps and illustrations so that the user can plan and complete a successful and safe trip or expedition – be it a long face climb, a walk over Lakeland fells, an alpine traverse, a Himalayan trek or a ramble in the countryside.

With a thorough introduction to assist planning, clear diagrams, maps and colour photographs to illustrate the terrain and route, and accurate and detailed text, Cicerone guides are designed for ease of use and access to the information.

If the facts on the ground change, or there is any aspect of a guide that you think we can improve, we are always delighted to hear from you.

Cicerone Press, 2 Police Square, Milnthorpe, Cumbria LA7 7PY
Tel 01539 562 069   Fax 01539 563 417
email info@cicerone.co.uk   web: www.cicerone.co.uk

CICERONE